YOUNG READERS'

PICTUREBOOK

OF

TAR HEEL AUTHORS

Fifth Edition, Revised

By

Richard Walser
and
Mary Reynolds Peacock

Raleigh
North Carolina Department of Cultural Resources
Division of Archives and History
1981

First Edition, 1957 .... 5,000 copies
Second Edition, 1960 .... 5,000 copies
    Additional Printing, 1963 .... 5,000 copies
Third Edition, 1966 .... 8,000 copies
Fourth Edition, 1975 .... 3,000 copies
Fifth Edition, 1981 .... 5,000 copies

DEPARTMENT OF CULTURAL RESOURCES

SARA W. HODGKINS
Secretary

DIVISION OF ARCHIVES AND HISTORY

WILLIAM S. PRICE
Acting Director

NORTH CAROLINA HISTORICAL COMMISSION

T. HARRY GATTON
Acting Chairman

FOREWORD

In 1957 the first edition of YOUNG READERS' PICTUREBOOK OF TAR HEEL AUTHORS was published by what was then known as the State Department of Archives and History. Since that time, as other editions have been issued, changes have been made in the text so as to keep information up to date and to provide biographical sketches of current authors. This fifth edition differs greatly from the fourth, published in 1975.

It is always difficult to select writers for inclusion. As was true of earlier versions of this publication, well-known literary figures from North Carolina's colonial period and from the late eighteenth and the nineteenth centuries have been included to provide historical perspective. Modern writers whose works are available in most school libraries have been selected, but many who were popular a few years ago have been dropped from the fifth edition to permit inclusion of others whose names are respected for their recent work. It is regrettable that space limitations prevent continuation of all authors of the past, many of whom produced outstanding novels, short stories, poems, and works of nonfiction. Many were excluded because they write primarily for adults.

Students interested in knowing more about the figures included in this small booklet will want to consult the bibliography included on the inside back cover.

Richard Walser, whose own writings are well known by thousands of schoolchildren and their parents, was joined in preparation of this new edition by Mary Reynolds Peacock, historical publications editor on the staff of the Division of Archives and History. Mrs. Peacock revised George B. Cutten's *Silversmiths of North Carolina*, a new edition of which was published in 1973. She has worked with numbers of editors and authors whose books were published by the Division of Archives and History. Assistance in typing was given by Henri Dawkins and in proofreading by Patricia R. Johnson, both members of the Historical Publications Section staff.

Memory F. Mitchell
Historical Publications Administrator

February 2, 1981

CONTENTS

THOMAS HARIOT

wrote the first North Carolina book. It was, incidentally, the first book in the English language written by one who had lived in what is now the United States. Published in London in 1588, its forty-eight pages are known by the strangely worded title *A briefe and true report of the new found land of Virginia.* It is, of course, about Roanoke Island, known to Englishmen of that day as the colony of Virginia. A reprint of Hariot's little volume is included in *Explorations, Descriptions, and At-* *tempted Settlements of Carolina, 1584-1590,* edited by David Leroy Corbitt.

Hariot gathered the notes for his pamphlet during the year he spent as a member of Sir Walter Raleigh's first colony on Roanoke, 1585-1586. When he returned to England, he wished to inform Sir Walter's friends of the most favorable aspects of this country beyond the seas. He wrote of the products which could be exported and sold in England: silkworms, flax, and hemp; pitch, tar, rosin, and turpentine; cedars, grapes, walnut oils, furs, deerskins, civet cats, copper, dyes, and pearls. He did not mention gold. Then Hariot told about those products which could be used by the colonists themselves: corn, peas, melons, roots, chestnuts, walnuts, grapes, and strawberries; squirrels, rabbits, and bears; oysters and fish. Tobacco (called *upponwoc*) is written about in detail. The third section, and most readable, describes the Indians, whom he found hospitable. All in all, Hariot's *Virginia* is a beguiling account.

In his own day Hariot was best known as a scientist. A native of Oxford, England, where he was born in 1560, he graduated from the university there and became Raleigh's tutor in mathematics. Then when the first colonists under Ralph Lane and Richard Grenville were being chosen, Raleigh asked Hariot to be the surveyor, naturalist, and historian of the group. Back in England, he remained in the service of Raleigh and was able to continue his scientific studies. In astronomy and algebra, he was far ahead of his times. But Hariot neglected to publish his experiments, and today he is best remembered for his slender little report on the Roanoke Island colony. He died at Isleworth near London in 1621. The portrait on this page, though unauthenticated, is believed to be Hariot's.

wrote a book called *A New Voyage to Carolina*, though in some editions it is known as Lawson's *History of North Carolina*. It was first published in 1709 and, like Hariot's *Virginia*, was intended to lure colonists and financial backers to the undeveloped land. Actually it is no history at all, but a volume of travels, descriptions, and Indian customs. What is more important is that it is written in a lively, good-humored style and makes delightful reading today.

No portrait of Lawson is known to exist. The picture on this page is a reproduction of an old woodcut illustrating Lawson's capture by the Indians just before his death in 1711. In his narrow-brimmed hat, he stands at Baron von Graffenried's left shoulder. Lawson was surveyor general of the colony, and the baron was leader to the Palatines who had settled New Bern the year before. With the baron's slave, the two were on a trip to the backcountry, where they were captured by the Tuscaroras. The Indians thought that Lawson's surveying had something to do with the seizure of their land. Though the baron managed to be set free, Lawson and the slave were put to death near the present town of Snow Hill—probably by having pine splinters stuck into their flesh and then lighted.

Little is known of Lawson before he came to America. A Londoner, he arrived in Charleston in 1700 and set out for the hinterlands. His journey to the foothills of North Carolina, then eastward through what now would be Charlotte, Salisbury, Greensboro, Hillsborough, Raleigh, Goldsboro, and Greenville, is told about in his book. Many of his experiences with the Indians were exciting. He settled in Bath, North Carolina's first town, and became one of its incorporators in 1705. Later he went to London to have his book published and, while there, interested von Graffenried in bringing his Protestant settlers to the Neuse River. Lawson wrote that North Carolina had "the mildest and best established Government in the World" and that it

was "the Place where any Man may peaceably enjoy his own without being invaded by another: Rank and Superiority ever giving Place to Justice and Equity." It was such a "plentiful Country," he said, that the men became lazy and the women had to do all the work.

THOMAS BURKE

was a North Carolina governor during the American Revolution. Long before that, however, he was a poet. Born in Ireland about 1744, he was a lad of sixteen when he emigrated to Accomack County on the eastern shore of Virginia after some family trouble still undetermined. There he studied medicine, and there he practiced writing poetry. Often young Burke would put his rhymes into a private shorthand (much of it preserved but not yet deciphered), for he said he dreaded "the Idle Character of a Rhimer," which he thought would be his if the practical, hard-working settlers of America found out what he was doing. But when the hated Stamp Act was repealed in 1766, he could not restrain himself from dashing off a patriotic poem to be read at a celebration. Though he hoped the authorship would be concealed, his name became known and he was widely acclaimed for his inspiring lines. Thereafter, he freely circulated his poems, and many of them were published in the newspapers.

Burke turned to the study of law when his practice of medicine brought him little money. He moved to Norfolk and married. In 1772, after his health failed, he set up a law office in Hillsborough where, he wrote, the "Lands are fertile, the Water good, and the Climate moderate and healthy." Burke was a fiery patriot, and when troubles with England became desperate, he belligerently supported the American side. For most of four years he was in Philadelphia as member of the Continental Congress. He was elected governor in 1781 but only a few months later was captured by the tories and held prisoner. Upon his escape, he completed his term as governor. Burke died on December 2, 1783, and was buried at his plantation near Hillsborough.

Besides his patriotic poems, Burke wrote much verse on the sheer joy of living. Many gentle stanzas are devoted to the ladies, whom he called such names as Delia and Chloe. He could, however, when ruffled, sting his enemies with bitter rhymes.

Though he was never more than amateur, each of his efforts proves the pleasure he got from writing imaginatively. The complete *Poems of Governor Thomas Burke of North Carolina* (1961), printed in the style of the eighteenth century, is available from the publishers of this PICTUREBOOK.

WILLIAM GASTON

was a noted statesman and a justice of the state supreme court. In 1835 he wrote the words for "The Old North State," which the legislature made the official patriotic song in 1927. The opening lines are well known:

> Carolina! Carolina! Heaven's blessing attend her!
> While we live we will cherish, protect and defend her.
> Though the scorner may sneer at and witlings defame her,
> Our hearts swell with gladness whenever we name her.
> Hurrah! Hurrah! the Old North State forever!
> Hurrah! Hurrah! the good old North State!

There are four other verses. It is said that Gaston composed the words to fit the tune of a melody played by a group of Swiss bell-ringers. Its first public hearing was at a political convention in Raleigh, October 6, 1840.

Judge Gaston was a gentleman-poet. Rarely did he write for the purpose of publication. However, he was quite gifted in dashing off appropriate lines for any occasion. May Day at the school, the death of a pet mockingbird, birthdays, the gift of a lady's glove—all called forth some poetic expression. Quite a few of his verses are preserved in Mary Bayard Clarke's *Woodnotes* (2 volumes, 1854), the first anthology of North Carolina poetry.

William Gaston was one of the most prominent men in North Carolina during the early nineteenth century. A county and a city are named for him. Born at New Bern in 1778, he attended schools near his home and, being a Catholic, went to Georgetown University in Washington. He studied law under François-Xavier Martin in New Bern after graduating from Princeton. He served eminently in the General Assembly of North Carolina and the Congress of the United States before ascending to the supreme court. He opposed slavery, and he is sometimes called "The Father of Religious Liberty in North Carolina" because he sponsored legislation allowing Catholics as well as Protestants to hold state offices. He died in 1844. Both his home and his law office are historic spots in New Bern today, and his grave may be visited in Cedar Grove Cemetery there.

GEORGE MOSES HORTON

was, unlike Burke and Gaston, a professional poet who supported himself during most of his life partly from the sale of his work. He was born a slave in Northampton County about 1797, the property of William Horton. After his master moved to a Chatham County plantation eight miles below Chapel Hill, the Negro boy, though he could not read or write, began composing poems in his head to the meter of hymns he had heard in church. Students at the university village, on his trips there to sell farm products, heard him recite; and soon they commissioned him to write love poems to be dispatched to their sweethearts back home. For such tasks he charged 25 to 75 cents. The students and the faculty gradually taught him to read and write, and influential citizens agitated a campaign to purchase his freedom. When their plans did not mature, Horton arranged to "hire out his time"; that is, he paid his master from his poetry money for the privilege of leaving the farm and living in Chapel Hill. If student purses were empty, he either got a job as janitor at the university or returned to his farm labors.

During his lifetime, three books of his were published: *The Hope of Liberty* (1829), *Poetical Works* (1845), and *Naked Genius* (1865). Protesting his status as a slave, *The Hope of Liberty* was the first book by a Negro in the South. All three volumes contain many love poems written for the beloved students, but there also are political and philosophical verses and a number of humorous selections. Horton called himself an "illiterate genius."

In 1865, when Union troops invaded North Carolina, the old slave escaped to their lines and was free at last. For the northern soldiers, he wrote poems just as he had for his college students, and a Yankee captain helped him in the publication of his final book. Horton moved to Philadelphia and for a while was quite a celebrity there. But life in the North was not so easy-going as in the South, and soon he had to seek other means of livelihood. He died about 1883, the place and date uncertain. Horton and Charles W. Chesnutt (see page 12) are the two most noted Negro authors from North Carolina. The drawing on this page is imaginary.

ROBERT STRANGE

was the author of *Eoneguski* (1839), a novel of the Cherokee Indians. In the state's literary history, it is important as the first novel written by a resident of North Carolina with scenes almost entirely within the borders of the state. Earlier writers of fiction had treated the state very sparingly. Strange felt that North Carolina history, customs, and people could provide stories as exciting and interesting as those about other areas. And he was right. Robert Strange was thus the first of a long line of distinguished authors who in North Carolina found thrilling events and characters which could be remade into fiction. Like Gaston, though, he was not primarily a literary man; rather, he was a hard-working lawyer who considered authorship a gentleman's pastime. He once said, "In literary pursuits I should be as happy as this world can make me" and added that the practice of law was a "dry technical profession." If Strange had lived a hundred years later, he might have been the professional writer of many books, instead of only one.

Eoneguski, or The Cherokee Chief, available to modern readers in a facsimile edition published in 1960, is a novel based on actual characters and events. After white settlers went beyond the Blue Ridge, they soon were in contact with the Indians, who resented further inroads on their hunting grounds. Seeking to be friends with the pioneering Americans, the Cherokee under Eoneguski (or Yonaguski) fought with Andrew Jackson against the Creek in 1814. In spite of that, treaties took more and more land from the Cherokee. Strange's book, a historical novel similar to Cooper's *The Last of the Mohicans,* clearly condemns the shabby treatment of the Indians by the whites.

Strange was born in Manchester, Virginia, in 1796, and graduated from Hampden-Sydney College in that state. At the age of nineteen, he moved to Fayetteville and became a lawyer. As a political figure, he served as a member of the state House of Commons, as a superior court judge (gaining information for *Eoneguski* when he held court in the mountain counties), as a United States senator, and as a district solicitor. He died in 1854 and is buried at the family home, "Myrtle Hill," near Fayetteville.

wrote *The Impending Crisis of the South: How to Meet It,* which was more responsible for the Civil War than any other book except Harriet Beecher Stowe's *Uncle Tom's Cabin.* As an influence on national thought, it is matched only by one other North Carolina book, W. J. Cash's *The Mind of the South* (1941).

Helper (1829-1909), born and reared on a farm near Mocksville in Davie County, always said his father owned four slaves. Peter S. Ney, famous man of mystery, was one of his teachers. From 1848 until 1850 Helper worked in Michael Brown's print shop in Salisbury. When he was accused of stealing money from the print shop (he later confessed and repaid the $300), Helper left Salisbury and went west to prospect for gold. In his first book, *The Land of Gold: Reality versus Fiction* (1855), Helper described California in unfavorable terms. He advocated extending slavery, denounced "meddling abolishionists," and used statistics indiscriminately.

Two years later in 1857 Helper—now returned to the East—published his sensational *The Impending Crisis* in which he reversed many opinions he had voiced in *The Land of Gold.* Again using statistics to suit his own purposes, he sought to prove that slavery had made the South inferior to the North and should be abolished. He had no humanitarian motives. Indeed, he hated blacks and thought nonslaveholding farmers and white laborers were unfairly subjugated to slaveholders who controlled wealth, politics, and society in the South. Many poor white southerners could not read his book, and neither northerners nor southerners understood Helper's philosophy; nevertheless, it was incendiary propaganda, and over 100,000 copies were distributed by the Republican party in the 1860 presidential campaign.

Helper married Maria Luisa Rodriguez while he was serving in Buenos Aires in 1861 as a consul appointed by President Lincoln. His wife left Helper several years later and returned to South America, taking their only child. The author became deranged and committed suicide in 1909.

Other books by the erratic visionary Helper included *The Negroes in Negroland: The Negroes in America and Negroes Generally* (1868); *Nojoque: a Question for a Continent* (1867); *Noonday Exigencies in America* (1871); *Oddments of Andean Diplomacy* (1879); and *The Three Americas Railway* (1881).

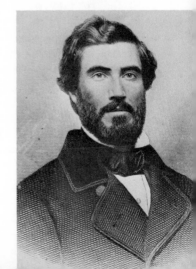

7

CALVIN HENDERSON WILEY

was a young lawyer (as this picture shows him) when he wrote two historical novels about North Carolina: *Alamance* (1847) and *Roanoke* (1849). Some years later he acquired fame as the first superintendent of common schools in North Carolina. But the two novels came first. They give Wiley the distinction of being the first *native* Tar Heel novelist. Good stories they are, too, though copies available to read are now quite rare.

Shortly before *Alamance* was published, Wiley wrote that he had always "cherished a desire to immortalize my old mother state." To do so, he planned a series of three novels on the three sections of North Carolina. *Alamance* was to tell of Revolutionary struggles in Guilford County between the whigs and tories of the Alamance Presbyterian Church community. A climax is provided in the Battle of Guilford Courthouse. For *Roanoke* he moved from the central part of the state to the east, and created his hero Walter Tucker, a democratic adventurer who wandered from Nags Head to Tryon's Palace in New Bern, and on to Wilmington and the Battle of Moores Creek Bridge. The third, which was to be about western North Carolina and was to be called *Buncombe*, was never written. After *Roanoke*, his literary career was considerably engulfed by other activities.

Wiley was born in 1819 at the family homestead three miles west of the Alamance Church near Greensboro. Following his graduation from the University of North Carolina at Chapel Hill, he settled in Oxford to practice law. There he found time to edit a newspaper and to write essays and novels. When his parents' poor health caused him to return to Guilford, he ran for the General Assembly and was elected. In Raleigh, Wiley fought for public schools and was then chosen to head a statewide system. Illiteracy was rampant everywhere in the state, and he compiled a *North Carolina Reader* (1851) for both the students and their parents. From 1852 to 1865 he traveled the state as superintendent of schools. The war brought his efforts to an end, and later he was secretary for the North Carolina Land Society and agent of the American Bible Society. Much of his educational and religious writing is uncollected. At the time of his death in 1887, he was a resident of Winston-Salem. Many public schools in North Carolina towns and cities are named for Wiley.

MARY ANN MASON

holds an important page in the literary history of North Carolina. Investigation shows that she was the first native Tar Heel to write a book for children. Thus it can be said that she opened up a field which has engaged the energy of many talented authors who have succeeded her. This book—*A Wreath from the Woods of Carolina* (1859)—is now sought after by collectors of rare books. It is doubtful if there are any copies available for student reading. But even if there were, young people today would find the ten little religious stories too syrupy for their taste. Each story uses a wild flower to teach a lesson on how to live. What particularly distinguishes the volume are nine handsome illustrations of wild flowers in color, painted by the author.

Among her other writings is a delightful book with this amazing title: *The Young Housewife's Counsellor and Friend, Containing Directions in every Department of Housekeeping Including the Duties of Wife and Mother* (1871). This guide, a sort of how-to-do-it book, contains not only delicious recipes but full information of what was expected of the lady of a southern home "before emancipation." *Her Church and Her Mother: a Story of Filial Piety* (1860) is a novel set in Raleigh. *The White Doe: A Legend of Olden Times* (1861, three installments in the *Raleigh Register*) is a fanciful short novel about Virginia Dare as a young woman.

Mary Ann Mason was a true daughter of the Old South. The wonder is that she found time to write at all. She was born in New Bern of prominent parentage in 1802. In 1823 she was married to Richard Sharpe Mason, Episcopal rector in her home town. For twelve years they lived in New York State and Delaware. Then in 1840 Dr. Mason came to Christ Church in Raleigh and remained there till his death. In the household were six children—and a niece, Mary Kinsey. Besides writing books, Mrs. Mason was skilled in painting, in botany, in cooking, in sculpture. For festive occasions she could model a ship out of big lumps of sugar for a centerpiece, and Mrs. Ben W. Baker of Raleigh owned a delicate cameo cut by Mary Ann Mason with an ordinary pen knife: an angel in brown and white illustrating a passage from Milton's *Paradise Lost*. All in all, Mrs. Mason was considered one of the most talented women in the state. She died in 1881.

CHRISTIAN REID

was one of the most popular American writers of light romance in the years following the Civil War. *The Land of the Sky* (1876), a well-known story of several young couples traveling about in the North Carolina mountains and having delightfully mild flirtations, gave to the western section of the state a nickname which it has borne ever since. Christian Reid wrote other stories of the Blue Ridge country, such as *A Summer Idyl* (1878) and *His Victory* (1887). Most of her forty-six books—a very impressive number—deal, however, with plantation and small-town life in the southern foothills; such a one is *Bonny Kate* (1878) and also *The Wargrave Trust* (1912). More than a dozen novels are set in the West Indies, Mexico, New York, and Europe. All are proper and decorous: the heroine may occasionally be self-willed but never coarse. Christian Reid wrote for an age which, like herself, believed in good taste and refinement.

Christian Reid was the pen name of Frances Fisher, born in Salisbury in 1846. Even at the age of three she invented lengthy tales which she related to her aunt. When her father, Colonel Charles Fisher, was killed in the opening months of the Civil War, she grew closer still to her maiden aunt, a Catholic, and soon embraced Catholicism. The war brought the family to an almost penniless situation; and Frances Fisher turned to writing for a livelihood. *Valerie Aylmer* (1870) was her first novel, written at the age of twenty-three. From then on, her course was clear. Novel after novel poured from her pen. In the South of those days, schoolteaching was the only respectable paying-job a *lady* could have. Modesty, therefore, demanded that Miss Fisher hide behind a pseudonym. She chose one which would conceal her sex and indicate the moral quality of her writing. Some years later, after great financial success, she was able to travel and live in Europe. In 1887 she married James M. Tiernan, a widower who owned silver mines in Mexico; there they lived for a

while. Following her husband's death, she remained in Salisbury, writing almost to the year of her death in 1920. In Salisbury today is a collection of her books and mementoes at the public library; a handsome stone tablet commemorates the memory of a beloved Christian woman and novelist. To her, fame was always secondary to character.

MARY BAYARD CLARKE

compiled the first anthology of North Carolina poetry, *Wood-Notes;
or Carolina Carols*, published in 1854 in Raleigh. In a day when no
southern ladies and few southern (no North Carolina) men were
professional writers, Mary Bayard Clarke earned much-needed
money for her family (there were four Clarke children) with her
poetry, book reviews, novelettes, travel sketches, reminiscences, and
translations. Equally important, she encouraged others to write and
then helped them to get their efforts published. Using the pen name
"Tenella," Mrs. Clarke in her introduction to *Wood-Notes* wrote:

"Come rouse you! ye poets of North Carolina
My State is my theme and I seek not a finer."

Mary Bayard Devereux, daughter of Thomas Pollock and Catherine
Anne Johnson Devereux, was born in Raleigh on May 13, 1827. An
English governess directed her education, using the same course out-
lined for her student's brother at Yale University. Mary Bayard
studied Spanish, Italian, French, and German. Much of the poetry
she later translated into English. Soon after her marriage to Major
William John Clarke, she accompanied him to Texas and Cuba; and
during the winter of 1854-1855 she was "queen of the small but select
group of English and Americans" living in Cuba. She espoused the
cause of the Confederacy during the Civil War, and much of her best
poetry reflects that enthusiasm. Her most active literary life,
however, came after the war when the family moved to New Bern in
1868. In a letter she wrote: "I am busy editing my paper, the *Literary
Pastime*; corresponding with two others; contributing to two
magazines; and translating a French novel; added to which I am composing the libretto for an opera, and writing Sunday-school hymns at
five dollars apiece." All this industry, however, took its toll. Mrs.
Clarke, always frail, died on March 30, 1886. The best of her poems
were edited by her friend Winchester Hall in
1905.

Much biographical material about Mary
Bayard Devereux Clarke can be found in her
sister's diary (*"Journal of a Secesh Lady"*: *The
Diary of Catherine Ann Devereux Edmondston,
1860-1866*. Edited by Beth Gilbert Crabtree and
James W. Patton. [Raleigh: North Carolina
Department of Cultural Resources, Division of
Archives and History, 1979]).

11

CHARLES W. CHESNUTT

was North Carolina's most prominent Negro author. At a time when others of his race in America were rather indifferent to literature, Chesnutt made a name for himself in open competition with the best of the white authors. Unfortunately, most of his novels and books of short stories are out of print today. Rare copies are sought by collectors. It would be helpful if some enterprising publisher would reissue a few of the titles.

Before the Civil War, Chesnutt's North Carolina parents went to Cleveland, Ohio, to live. Their son was born on June 20, 1858. During the war his father served in the Federal forces but later returned to Fayetteville, where young Charles was educated. At fourteen he sold a serial story to a Negro newspaper and his career was launched. At sixteen he was teaching in the Charlotte public schools. At twenty-two he was principal of the State Normal School in Fayetteville. But the discouraging days of Reconstruction in North Carolina were not favorable for the advancement of a clever young light-complexioned man of ambition like Chesnutt. He rightly resented the blocks in his pathway. So in 1883 he was again in the North, briefly in New York as a newspaperman and then permanently in Cleveland. In the great Ohio city he was respected as a court reporter, stenographer, lawyer, lecturer, and public-spirited citizen. During the few years of his writing activity he never lacked for support; Mark Twain, William Dean Howells, North Carolina's Walter Hines Page, Booker T. Washington, and others admired and advised him. He died in 1932.

Never during those long years in Cleveland did he forget North Carolina, for love of one's parental land overcomes prejudice. Practically all of his books deal with the racial difficulties in the Cape Fear country. Believing in the equality of man, he was the first Negro who dared to deal with the "color line," that segment of society with mixed blood. Three novels and a volume of short stories explore the angles of racial antagonism. It is a curious twist, certainly, that these books are far less remembered than *The Conjure Woman* (1899), dialect stories of slavery days told by an old Negro to his northern patron.

THOMAS DIXON, JR.

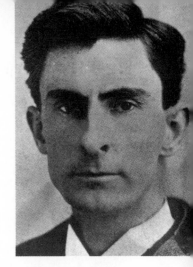

said in 1934: "I have written twenty-two novels, nine plays, and six motion pictures. I have made millions of dollars and lived it up and lost it, and find myself penniless at the age of seventy." The novels which first brought him money and fame were *The Leopard's Spots: A Romance of the White Man's Burden* (1902) and *The Clansman: An Historical Romance of the Ku Klux Klan* (1905). These two books, artless but never dull, portrayed Reconstruction in North Carolina as Dixon remembered it from boyhood. He despised slavery but preached white supremacy. *The Clansman* was made into a sensational stage play in 1905 and, as *The Birth of a Nation* a decade later, became the first mammoth silent film in Hollywood history. It was and remains today a classic motion picture.

Born near Shelby in 1864, Dixon graduated from Wake Forest in 1883 and was elected to the legislature before he could vote. Amazingly versatile, he achieved success as a lawyer, Baptist preacher, actor, lecturer, playwright, movie producer, and real estate promoter. However, he failed dismally and lost a fortune in his avantgarde effort to establish a colony for intellectuals in the mountains of North Carolina. After 1937 he was for a time clerk of the federal court in Raleigh.

Dixon's law career was abandoned when he became a preacher in Boston and New York. Then he turned to lecturing as a means of popularizing his ideas. Deciding that novels would be more effective, Dixon began to write. *The Leopard's Spots*, with its theme of Reconstruction, was predictably provocative and popular. *The Flaming Sword* (1939), Dixon's last novel, had a similar effect inasmuch as it dealt with a later but equally controversial subject, the dangers of Communism in America. Other volatile subjects used in Dixon's novels included woman's rights, religion, and politics. He was forceful, bold, and emotional in his writing.

Twice married—first to Harriet Bussey and after her death to Madelyn Donovan—Dixon died in 1946 and was buried in Shelby. His racial prejudices are generally viewed today as completely unacceptable, but the energetic, imaginative man who created *The Clansman* was the product of his time, and his work has commanded an enormous readership. *The Birth of a Nation* had an unparalleled impact on the motion picture industry.

OLIVE TILFORD DARGAN

was a triple-genre writer. First, she excelled in poetic drama. Then, perhaps realizing that such plays were passé, she turned to lyric poetry. Still later, she moved into prose fiction as a means of expressing her sympathy for the less fortunate. At times the three kinds of literature were explored simultaneously. Born on January 11, 1869, in Grayson County, Kentucky, the young girl in 1879 moved with her parents to Missouri where the elder Tilfords were to teach in a small school. Their aide three years later was thirteen-year-old Olive. After receiving a degree from Peabody College in 1888 she taught in Arkansas, Texas, and Nova Scotia before studying at Radcliffe, 1893-1894. There she met a Harvard senior, Pegram Dargan of South Carolina, whom she married in 1898. After eight years of residence in New York, the Dargans in 1906 seized the opportunity to move to Horizon Farm, a country place near Almond in Swain County. Even after her husband drowned in 1915, the writer lived at the farm until 1925 when she moved to Asheville.

Semiramis and Other Plays (1904) was followed by *Lords and Lovers, and Other Dramas* (1906) and *The Flutter of the Gold Leaf and Other Plays* (1922; with Frederick Peterson). *Pathfinder* (1914), her first book of poetry, was praised highly. *The Cycle's Rim* (1916), a collection of fifty-three sonnets dedicated to her late husband, won the $500 prize given by the Southern Society of New York for the best book of the year by a southern writer. *Lute and Furrow* (1922) contains lyrical verse which sings of her love for the mountains as does *The Spotted Hawk* (1958), winner of the 1959 Roanoke-Chowan Poetry Award.

Three novels were published under the pseudonym Fielding Burke. Her sympathy for textile workers involved in the Gastonia strike of 1929 is evident in *Call Home the Heart* (1932) and *A Stone Came Rolling* (1935). A third novel, *Sons of the Stranger* (1947), is about western miners.

Asheville Citizen-Times

Some of Mrs. Dargan's best writing is to be found in her short stories and sketches. *The Welsh Pony* was published in 1913; *From My Highest Hill* came in 1941; *Innocent Bigamy and Other Stories* (1962) was her last publication.

One of the greatest of many honors came to Olive Tilford Dargan in 1925 when she was awarded a doctor of letters degree by the University of North Carolina. She died in 1968 at the age of ninety-nine.

14

O. HENRY

is the pen name of William Sidney Porter, one of America's most popular writers of short stories. He was born near Greensboro in 1862. When he was only three, his mother died and he was left in the care of his father, a doctor. He grew up under the watchful eye of his Aunt Lina Porter, who conducted a private school attended by Will and the other children of the neighborhood. It was all the education he had. Soon he was working in an uncle's drug store, and eventually he became a registered pharmacist. But life in the village of Greensboro was humdrum, and when he received an invitation to go to Texas he accepted. At nineteen he was tramping about a huge ranch operated by some friends from North Carolina. In spite of his shy nature, he always had friends. In Austin he settled down as a bank clerk and was married. There was one daughter. At odd moments he ventured a humorous weekly newspaper, the *Rolling Stone*, but it was never successful. Just how it all happened is not quite clear, but at this time his accounts at the bank were found to be unbalanced and he was charged with embezzlement. To escape trial he sailed to Honduras. His wife's tuberculosis became worse; and when he returned some months later, he stood trial and was sent to the Ohio Penitentiary. There he began writing in earnest and sold some stories. On his release, he resolved to start life anew, even to changing his name. Many stories are told of why he chose O. Henry (see Gerald Langford's biography *Alias O. Henry*), probably all of them containing some bit of truth. At any rate, he went to New York and soon was the most widely read author in the nation. His powers of plot-invention were spectacular. For instance, during 1904-1905 he produced for the *Sunday World* a story a week. O. Henry's stories of New York City are favorites among student readers. About North Carolina he wrote little. Two of the best-known stories are "A Blackjack Bargainer" and "Let Me Feel Your Pulse," the first about a Blue Ridge Mountain feud, the second a partially autobiographical incident from his Weaverville days.

Dictionary of American Portraits

His second marriage was to Sara Coleman of Weaverville. He died in 1910 and is buried in Asheville.

PHILLIPS RUSSELL

like many other authors in North Carolina, combined writing and teaching. He was born in Rockingham, August 5, 1884. After graduating from the University of North Carolina at Chapel Hill, where he had edited several campus publications, he worked with newspapers and magazines in Charlotte, New York, Chicago, and Philadelphia. Beginning in 1921, he was the only American on the staff of a London newspaper. During his four years in London, he wrote numerous stories and articles and published two little books of poems. By 1925 he was back in New York working on several biographies based on fresh material he had found in England and France. In 1931 he was invited to join the English Department at Chapel Hill, and in the same year he married Caro Mae Green, sister of the dramatist Paul Green. From 1936 until his retirement in 1956, he taught in the Department of Journalism there. In the late 1950s he edited a Chapel Hill newspaper. Meanwhile he had bought a farm in nearby Chatham County, where he did all of the work himself. However, he continued to live in Chapel Hill until his death on November 20, 1974.

Benjamin Franklin, the First Civilized American (1926) was followed by *John Paul Jones, Man of Action* (1927), biography of the naval hero who began his career in North Carolina. *Emerson, the Wisest American* (1929) and *William the Conqueror* (1933) evinced the breadth of Phillips Russell's interests, as did *Harvesters* (1932), biographical essays on seven men influential in history. *The Glittering Century* (1936) is a study of eighteenth-century Europe. He won the Mayflower Cup with *The Woman Who Rang the Bell* (1949), biography of his great-aunt Cornelia Phillips Spencer, who was a mighty force for progress in North Carolina in the tragic years after the Civil War. *Jefferson, Champion of the Free Mind* (1956), was, like his books on Franklin and Emerson, the biography of an American intellectual. In late 1965 he published *North Carolina in the Revolutionary War.* Two books are quite unlike his other titles: *Fumbler* (1928) is a novel of a small-town editor, and *Red Tiger* (1929) traces his travels in Yucatan and Mexico. *These Old Stone Walls* (1972) is a book about Chapel Hill.

Russell won the North Carolina Award in 1968. Robert Ruark, one of his pupils, once said that Phillips Russell "taught writing for the love of it."

HUGH T. LEFLER

Portrait: William Fields

is a man most people think of when the subject of North Carolina history is brought up. With Dr. A. R. Newsome as coauthor, he brought out a school history, *The Growth of North Carolina* (1942), and a one-volume survey for adults, *North Carolina: The History of a Southern State* (1954). The latter, which won the Mayflower Cup for excellence in nonfiction by a North Carolinian, was revised in 1963 and again in 1973. His two-volume *North Carolina* (1956) contains a half million words. Next was an updating of his school history, now titled *North Carolina: History, Geography, Government* (1959, 1966). Yet Dr. Lefler says that the history of North Carolina is only his secondary interest, that he is first of all a student of colonial America. After his retirement in 1973, he collaborated with William S. Powell in writing the authoritative *Colonial North Carolina* (1973).

Lefler was born on a Davie County farm in 1901. Until he graduated from nearby Cooleemee High School, he worked on the farm and loved it. From Weaver College (now closed) he went to Trinity (Duke) for A.B. and M.A. degrees. In college he won monograms in basketball, track, baseball, and tennis. After a year teaching history at Greensboro High School, he went to the University of Pennsylvania, from which he received the Ph.D. degree in 1931. Meanwhile he had begun teaching at North Carolina State University, where he was head of the Department of History. In 1935 he went to the University of North Carolina at Chapel Hill where his classes in North Carolina history became among the most popular on the campus. When not writing history, which Dr. Lefler does for several hours before breakfast each morning, he plays golf and tends his vegetable garden.

Historical theories do not interest Hugh T. Lefler overmuch. His one passion is a passion for truth. Unless a fact can be proved conclusively, it does not go into his books. As a result, he has often been called a "debunker," that is, one who has no use for legends or commonly accepted beliefs when passed off as history. For instance, he carefully points out that Virginia Dare was not the first white child born in what is now the United States. "She was merely the first English child, for the Spanish were in Florida years before."

JAMES LARKIN PEARSON

was commissioned Poet Laureate of North Carolina by Governor William B. Umstead on August 4, 1953, during impressive ceremonies in the House of Representatives at the State Capitol in Raleigh. The honor was the climax to a long and full life devoted to poetry. Pearson's story is the story of "the little boy who wanted to run for poet—instead of president." Finally in 1953 he had won the position he wished for most. It all began when he was four years old. He was riding with his father one winter day. "Getting cold?" he was asked. His reply came: "My fingers and my toes—my feet and my hands—are just as cold as—you ever see'd a man's."

He was born September 13, 1879, in a one-room cabin on Berry's Mountain near Boomer in Wilkes County. The hill people of the section were not prosperous, and young Larkin had little schooling. Off and on he would attend the one-teacher free school and when he was sixteen quit entirely. But the urge to put words into rhyme was always there. He read whatever books he could find, especially those by poets, and at twelve years of age was trying seriously to write. Until he was twenty-one, he worked on the farm. "I always carried my notebook and pencil to the field with me," he explains, "and as I trudged between the plowhandles in the hot sunshine my mind was busy working out a poem. On reaching the end of the furrow I would stop and write down what I had composed. In this way most of my early poems were produced." Later he went over the mountain to Jefferson and learned printing, which, besides writing poetry, has been his vocation ever since. As printer and editor of various small county newspapers, he had some success. He was married, and times looked bright. After his wife and his father died in 1934, he remained at "Fifty Acres" in Wilkes County for five years. In 1939 he married Eleanor Louise Fox and went to live at her home in the village of Guilford College. Since her death in 1962, he has lived in North

Wilkesboro. The James Larkin Pearson Building is located on the campus of Wilkes Community College.

Of Pearson's first five books, all collectors' items since they were printed by him on his own press, *Fifty Acres* (1937) is best known. Both *The Collected Poems of James Larkin Pearson* (1960) and *"My Fingers and My Toes"* (1971) contain new poems as well as old favorites.

18

JOHN CHARLES McNEILL

is a poet much beloved by North Carolina readers. Born July 26, 1874, near what is now the village of Wagram, he grew up on his father's farm there. He thoroughly enjoyed his boyhood in the country: fishing, going to church, hunting 'possums, swimming in the river, helping on the farm, talking with the Negroes, "holding off the calf" at milking time, tramping the woods. All these pleasant pastimes he later wrote into lines of verse which are on some occasions delightfully humorous, on others quite serious.

As a youth, he was an avid reader in a home where books were constantly being discussed. Studies were easy. At Wake Forest College he began writing poems—immature efforts though they were—while making a brilliant record in the classroom. He edited the *Wake Forest Student* for two years, was granted a license to practice law, and graduated in 1898 as valedictorian. In the fall he returned to Wake Forest, was instructor in English, and earned a master's degree. Then he taught English at Mercer University in Georgia but left in 1900 to set up a law office in Lumberton for a year and then in Laurinburg. But law was not a suitable profession for McNeill. The only side of it he really enjoyed was a "Negro fight" case, when he could study the character he loved and put him into verse. Often he would simply shut up his office and go fishing. Even at his desk, he would frequently lock his doors and pull the shades on his windows and pour upon paper the poetry which was gushing from within him. In 1904 he was invited to join the *Charlotte Observer* staff. He did so willingly, for it gave him the opportunity to write at leisure. The next three years were his most productive. He died in 1907 and is buried at the old Spring Hill Cemetery in Scotland County.

McNeill's poetry seems timeless in its appeal. *Songs Merry and Sad* (1906) are easily understood short selections by a home-loving, warmhearted poet. *Lyrics from Cotton Land* (1907) contains dialect verse, mostly humorous. *Possums and Persimmons*

Engraving, E. G. Williams and Bro.

(1977) is a volume of previously uncollected poems edited by Richard Walser. "Possum Time" may have inspired the book's title:

> De 'simmons soon be yaller,
>   En de blaggum berries blue
> Does you need to ax a feller
>   Wut 'e's gwine a-do?

19

INGLIS FLETCHER

purchased one-hundred-and-fifty-year-old Bandon Plantation in 1944 and lived there till it was destroyed by fire in 1963. Nine miles north of Edenton, which is the scene of so many of her historical novels, Bandon provided her with the quiet needed for a writer.

There at Bandon she wrote all but the first few books of the impressive Carolina Series—twelve novels which explore early North Carolina in the readable guise of fiction, from the Roanoke Island settlements to the ratification of the Constitution in 1789. Though in the 1930s she had published two African novels based on a safari she made to Nyasaland in 1928, she was inspired to write about North Carolina (which she had never visited) as she searched for information about her Tyrrell County forebears. *Raleigh's Eden* (1940) was followed by *Men of Albemarle* (1942); *Lusty Wind for Carolina* (1944), a story of pirates; *Toil of the Brave* (1946); *Roanoke Hundred* (1948), about Raleigh's first colony in 1585; *Bennett's Welcome* (1950); *Queen's Gift* (1952); *The Scotswoman* (1955), about Flora Macdonald; *The Wind in the Forest* (1957); *Cormorant's Brood* (1959); *Wicked Lady* (1962); and *Rogue's Harbor* (1964). Edenton and the Albemarle Sound area, in at least eight of the series, have given Mrs. Fletcher more than an abundance of facts, events, and even characters for her historical novels. Much about how she went about research and writing can be found in her autobiography, *Pay, Pack and Follow* (1959).

Minna Inglis Clark was born October 20, 1879, in Alton, Illinois, of North Carolina and New York stock. After classes in sculpture at the St. Louis School of Fine Arts, she married John G. Fletcher, mining engineer. The couple went off immediately to remote mining camps in California and Alaska, then lived in Spokane and San Francisco during the boyhood of their son Stuart. After settling in North Carolina, Mrs. Fletcher involved herself in the state's cultural activities. She won the Sir Walter Raleigh Award in 1953 for the total of her work, not just for one book, and was honored with the North Carolina Award in 1964. She died in Edenton on May 30, 1969. She and John G. Fletcher are buried in the National Cemetery at Wilmington.

JAMES BOYD

brought fame to himself and to North Carolina with *Drums* (1925), a Revolutionary War historical novel about a piney-woods lad who, after his conviction that the American cause was just, served under John Paul Jones against the British. Wallace Irwin pointed out that Boyd's "historical characters are not just costumed actors. They stand out, forthright men and women, and talk to you in a language not far different from our own today. Why should they be so different? They are people of Carolina's farms, hills and streams." In a way, *Drums* was a new thing in fiction: a realistic (not a romantic) historical novel. It has now earned a permanent spot in the pages of American letters.

Its author was born in Dauphin County, Pennsylvania, in 1888. As a lad, he spent his holidays in Southern Pines where his grandfather had settled. His early interest in literature led to his majoring in English at Princeton and a continuation of this study at Cambridge University, England. During World War I, he participated in front-line action in Europe. The battle injuries he received were complicated by a persistent sinus infection. In 1919 he moved with his family to Southern Pines—mainly because he loved it as his boyhood home and because he wanted to try to write about the state's early days. Boyd was a constant reader, especially of poetry, and a tireless researcher. There was within him the need for knowledge and perfection—qualities which are obvious in his writings. In Southern Pines he set to work with dead seriousness. He built a house on the ridge above the town and in jollier moments entertained his friends, served as Master of the Moore County Hounds, and took part in various community and state activities. The novels came along. In 1941 he purchased the *Pilot*, a Southern Pines newspaper, and wrote for it. In 1944 he died suddenly in Princeton, where he had been hard at work in the library.

Besides *Drums*, titles of particular interest to North Carolina students are *Marching On* (1927), an exciting novel of the Lower Cape Fear country during the Civil War; *Long Hunt* (1930), tale of the westward movement from North Carolina into Tennessee; and *Old Pines and Other Stories* (1952), a posthumous collection of his short stories.

PAUL GREEN

is best known for those plays of his which are given each summer in huge outdoor theaters: *The Lost Colony* (since 1937) at Manteo; *The Stephen Foster Story* (1959) at Bardstown, Kentucky; *Cross and Sword* (1965) at St. Augustine, Florida; and *Texas* (1966) at Palo Duro Canyon State Park, Texas. Other "symphonic dramas," combining music and dancing and history with a fictitious plot, have appeared in Fayetteville, in Virginia Beach, in Williamsburg, in Washington, D.C., in Florida, Ohio, and California. Yet these sixteen plays, for which he invented the formula, represent only one phase of a varied writing career.

Born on a farm near Lillington in 1894, young Paul Green attended the local country schools, picked cotton, and played baseball. At nineteen, after graduating at Buies Creek, he became principal of a small school in his native Harnett County and earned enough money to pay his tuition to the University of North Carolina, which he entered as a freshman in 1916. Service in World War I interrupted his college career; and when he returned to Chapel Hill he began, under the inspiration of "Proff" Koch, to write short folk plays about the Negroes and the white farmers he had known as a boy. Soon he advanced to the full-length play. *In Abraham's Bosom* (1927), the tragedy of a Negro schoolmaster, won the Pulitzer Prize for the most distinguished American drama of the year. Other plays of the southern scene were produced in New York. Meanwhile he had married and was teaching philosophy at the university. After a Guggenheim Fellowship, which took him to Europe to study the exciting theater experiments going on there, he returned home and wrote dramas which added such elements as music, ballet, pantomime, and poetry to his folk themes. The plays of this period, like *Johnny Johnson* and *Roll, Sweet Chariot*, are fascinating productions.

Paul Green has published two novels, several volumes of short

Lavergne

stories, and many other books. He has often been in Hollywood, writing for the motion pictures. As a "cultural ambassador," he has represented the United States in Europe and Asia. In 1952 he won the first Sir Walter Raleigh Award for outstanding work in fiction by a North Carolinian and in 1965 was presented the North Carolina Award. The Paul Green Theater on the university campus at Chapel Hill was dedicated in 1978. Now he devotes his entire time to literature.

FREDERICK H. KOCH

was not a writer so much as a teacher of writers. In 1918, when he came to North Carolina, the state was hardly a producer of books. True, the raw materials for novels and poems and dramas were here, but few literary artists were using them. Most of the Tar Heel writers, like Chesnutt and O. Henry, had gone north. The home-staying group, sad to say, did not represent high standards. Along with other helpful influences, however, Koch changed all that. In his playwriting classes at Chapel Hill, young talent began to assert itself. Koch told his students: "Do not search for characters and plots in distant lands. Right back there in your hometown are people and events which will make a play. Open your inner eye, and write down what you see." They did, and "Proff" (for so he was always called) guided their stumbling little one-act plays till they were ready to be produced on the Carolina Playmakers' stage. These were the Carolina *folk plays*.

Those who began to write under Proff's direction did not all turn out to be dramatists. Some switched to other types of writing, but all had their literary beginnings in his classes. In this PICTUREBOOK, Koch students are Bernice Kelly Harris, Paul Green, LeGette Blythe, Thomas Wolfe, Jonathan Daniels, Frances Gray Patton, and Betty Smith. Among others who have been prominent in the various fields of literature are Josefina Niggli, Foster Fitz-Simons, Lucy Cobb, Joseph Mitchell, Charles Edward Eaton, Noel Houston, and Walter Spearman. Samuel Selden succeeded Koch as director of the Carolina Playmakers.

Koch was born in Kentucky in 1877. After college years at Ohio Wesleyan University and Harvard, he went to teach at the University of North Dakota. There he organized the Dakota Playmakers to write and produce plays about the everyday people—the folk. This work he continued at the University of North Carolina. His writings are largely confined to a pageant, *Raleigh, the Shepherd of the Ocean* (1920) and to those excellent introductions in the many volumes of folk plays written by his students. He died in 1944. Fred Koch, Jr., one of his four sons, is also an accomplished teacher and director of college theater activities.

BERNICE KELLY HARRIS

was the first woman to win the Mayflower Cup. The book which was honored was *Purslane* (1939), her first adventure into publishing. It was the first novel about North Carolina people ever to receive a literary award anywhere. Yet *Purslane* is a strangely simple book. It concerns the lives of farming people in Wake County at the turn of the century: tobacco curing, cotton picking, hog killing, 'coon hunting, box suppers, Sunday School excursions, Christmas celebrations, church meetings, baseball games, and the like. Its excellence lies not so much in rapid plot or exciting events as in Mrs. Harris's accurate pictures of a definite time and place, and in her grasp of the warmth in human character.

Though a first novel, *Purslane* is a mature book, backed by many years of experience and preparation. Bernice Christiana Kelly was born on October 8, 1891, in the Mt. Moriah community twelve miles east of Raleigh. The farm, the country school, and the Baptist church were the centers of her childhood. After graduating from Meredith College, she taught school briefly at Beulaville and Maiden; she also taught at Seaboard in Northampton County, where she made her home. In the summer of 1919 she was in Chapel Hill studying playwriting under "Proff" Koch. First she showed her high school English students how to write plays, then tried a few of her own— with marked success. They were collected as *Folk Plays of Eastern Carolina* (1940). Following her marriage to Herbert Harris, who died in 1950, she gave up teaching school and began writing. In 1966 Governor Dan K. Moore presented to her a North Carolina Award for literary distinction.

Besides *Purslane*, there are six other novels, all set in Wake or Northampton County. *Portulaca* (1941) is about small-town life. *Sweet Beulah Land* (1943) and *Sage Quarter* (1945) are wistful stories of the countryside, and *Janey Jeems* (1946) recounts the history of a lovable Negro family. *Hearthstones* (1948), Mrs. Harris's only historical novel, was made into a play in 1957. *Wild Cherry Tree Road* (1951) is similar to *Purslane* in character and setting. Two seasonal gift books are *The Very Real Truth about Christmas* (1961) and *The Santa on the Mantel* (1964). *Southern Savory* (1964) is an autobiography. She died September 13, 1973, in Durham.

LeGETTE BLYTHE

is a versatile writer. He is equally skilled in drama, fiction, biography, and history.

While still a practicing newspaperman, he wrote *Marshal Ney: A Dual Life* (1937), the first of his twenty-four books. It is the biography of Napoleon's general who, according to legend, mysteriously escaped death by a firing squad and reportedly came to North Carolina in the guise of a country schoolmaster. Next was *Alexandriana* (1940), a historical novel of Revolutionary days in old Mecklenburg County. Then came a play, *Shout Freedom!* (1948), an outdoor historical drama produced in Charlotte. After that, it was "change about" almost every year. Blythe has written a series of successful Biblical novels on New Testament themes: *Bold Galilean* (1948), *A Tear for Judas* (1951), *The Crown Tree* (1957), *Hear Me, Pilate!* (1961), *Man on Fire* (1964), and *Brothers of Vengeance* (1969). Other plays are *The Chatham Rabbit*, acted by the Carolina Playmakers, and *Voice in the Wilderness* (1955), celebrating Presbyterian church history. *The Hornets' Nest* (1968) is an outdoor drama centering on the history of Mecklenburg County. *William Henry Belk: Merchant of the South* (1950) and *James W. Davis: North Carolina Surgeon* (1957) are other biographies. *Miracle in the Hills* (1953), a Mayflower Cup winner for nonfiction, is the story, told in her own words, of Dr. Mary Martin Sloop of Crossnore. Similar books are *Gift from the Hills* (1958), the story of Lucy Morgan's Penland School; *Thomas Wolfe and His Family* (1961), written with the novelist's sister, Mabel Wheaton; and *Mountain Doctor* (1964), with Dr. Gaine Cannon. *Call Down the Storm* (1958) is a strong novel with a racial theme.

LeGette Blythe was born in Huntersville, Mecklenburg County, in 1900. From private tutoring and public schools he entered the University of North Carolina at Chapel Hill and studied under Dr. Edwin Greenlaw, eminent teacher of English, and "Proff" Koch of the Carolina Playmakers. At Chapel Hill he was involved in every student publication on the campus. After a year of teaching in Greensboro, he went with the *Charlotte News* and, in 1927, with the *Charlotte Observer.* Not till 1950 did he give up journalism to devote his full time to creative writing. LeGette and Esther Farmer Blythe, who live in Huntersville, have two sons and a daughter.

GERALD W. JOHNSON

was the author of some three dozen books and an almost uncountable number of articles for magazines and reviews. Cousin of the poet John Charles McNeill, Gerald White Johnson was born in Riverton on August 6, 1890. After graduating from Wake Forest College and serving an unusual literary apprenticeship as lineman, store clerk, bank teller, and factory hand, he started a newspaper in Thomasville, later moved over to Lexington as a reporter for $10.00 a week, then wound up on the *Greensboro Daily News*. During World War I he was with the army in Europe, and after the armistice he attended the University of Toulouse in southern France. Following several more years with the Greensboro newspaper, he became a teacher of journalism in the university at Chapel Hill. From 1926 to 1943 he was with the *Sun* papers in Baltimore and continued to live there as a free-lance writer and news commentator until his death in March, 1980. Among his many honors was the North Carolina Award in 1965 for "his distinction as a man of letters."

Most of Johnson's books have to do with American politics and culture. His attitude, a critical one with a strong tinge of liberalism, is nevertheless colored by his belief that the "aggregate wisdom of the people . . . is greater than that of any one man or of any one group, including the intellectuals." Among his biographies of great Americans are those of Andrew Jackson (1927), Franklin D. Roosevelt (1941), Woodrow Wilson (1944), and John Paul Jones (1947). Two novels have settings in North Carolina: *By Reason of Strength* (1930) and *Number Thirty-Six* (1933). *Beware the Dog!* (1939) is a murder mystery written under the name Charles North, transliteration of his native North Carolina.

For his grandson Peter, born in 1950, he wrote a trilogy of American history: *America Is Born* (1959), *America Grows Up* (1960), and *America Moves Forward* (1960). Another group for ages ten to

Max Araujo

fourteen includes *The Presidency* (1962), *The Supreme Court* (1962), *The Congress* (1963), and *The Cabinet* (1966). Other books are *Communism: An American's View* (1964); *Franklin D. Roosevelt* (1967); and *The Imperial Republic* (1972).

JONATHAN DANIELS

is proof that the writing of books is something that runs in the blood. His mother was a distant cousin of O. Henry. His father, Josephus Daniels, the eminent newspaperman and political figure, managed to publish a multivolume autobiography as well as other works. His daughter, Lucy Daniels (Inman), prefers to write fiction. Midway between them, Jonathan Daniels has produced many different kinds of books, among them three biographies for young readers: *Stonewall Jackson* (1959), AAUW Award-winner for 1960; *Mosby, Gray Ghost of the Confederacy* (1959); and *Robert E. Lee* (1960). His plea for conservation in the South, *The Forest Is the Future* (1957), is a stock item in school libraries all over the region.

Jonathan Daniels was born in Raleigh on April 26, 1902. At the University of North Carolina at Chapel Hill he was with the Carolina Playmakers at the same time Paul Green, Thomas Wolfe, and LeGette Blythe were being initiated into creative literature by way of the folk drama. From Columbia University he received a law degree but never practiced seriously: tradition and the writing instinct were too strong to resist. His editorship of the Raleigh *News and Observer*, a newspaper noted for its liberal slant in a region basically conservative, extends from 1933, with time out in Washington for political assignments under Presidents Franklin D. Roosevelt and Harry S. Truman. Now editor emeritus, he lives in retirement at Hilton Head Island, South Carolina.

His list of titles is impressive. *A Southerner Discovers the South* (1938) and *A Southerner Discovers New England* (1940) were followed by *Tar Heels* (1941), still the best informal picture of North Carolinians ever written. *Frontier on the Potomac* (1946), *The Man of Independence* (1950), and *The End of Innocence* (1954) are inside looks at high-level politics. *Prince of Carpetbaggers* (1958) is an exposé of Reconstruction years in North Carolina. *Thomas Wolfe: October Recollections* (1961) was followed by *The Devil's Backbone* (1962), story of the famous Natchez Trace, and *They Will Be Heard* (1965), about crusading newspaper editors. Other important publications include *The Time between the Wars* (1966); *Ordeal of Ambition: Jefferson, Hamilton, Burr* (1970); *Eleanor and Franklin* (1971); and *White House Witness: 1942-1945* (1975). Jonathan Worth Daniels, presented the North Carolina Award in 1967, has twice won the Mayflower Cup for the excellence of his books.

27

THOMAS WOLFE

was born in Asheville in 1900. His mother was a woman of the mountains, his father a stonecutter from Pennsylvania. In public schools and later in a private academy, he observed carefully the life around him. He stored away in his mind the tens of thousands of impressions later to be used in the most impressive books ever written by a North Carolinian. The town of Asheville was just then expanding into a bustling resort. But young, tall Tom Wolfe was not satisfied. He was always looking out beyond the hills which he said "hemmed" him in. At fifteen he entered the University of North Carolina at Chapel Hill and, before his graduation, became one of the most important figures on the campus. Besides majoring in English, he worked for the college publications and studied playwriting under "Proff" Koch.

Determined on a career as a professional dramatist, he went to Harvard for a master's degree and, when his plays were not accepted immediately by Broadway producers, began teaching English at New York University. On a trip abroad he suddenly started writing out the vivid recollections of his boyhood in Asheville, which he called Altamont. The result was *Look Homeward, Angel* (1929), a novel that is one of the high marks of American fiction, one later made into a successful Broadway play. It tells of the experiences of a sensitive lad in a mountain town and later in college at Pulpit Hill (his name for Chapel Hill). Other long novels pursuing the career of their autobiographical hero are *Of Time and the River* (1935), *The Web and the Rock* (1939), and *You Can't Go Home Again* (1940). There are numerous books of short stories, plays, essays, poetic passages, and letters. Four of the dozens of studies concerning him and his work are listed inside the back cover of this PICTUREBOOK.

Look Homeward, Angel was quite successful on publication; so Wolfe, with the aid of a Guggenheim Fellowship, gave up his teaching post and went off to Europe to write. Thereafter, he lived for the most part in New York. He was never married. Particularly he wished to see all of the America he wrote about. On a trip to the Northwest he became ill and died on September 15, 1938, after a brain operation in Baltimore.

W. J. CASH

died at age 41 and wrote only one book. Yet that book, in which Cash attempted to define the southern character, is one of the most influential pieces of writing ever to come out of the South. *The Mind of the South* (1941) was the result of a decade of hard work accompanied by multitudinous frustrations. Only Cash, with his unique perception of forces that have made southerners "different," his obsession with the psyche of the South, and his compulsion to write it all down could have produced such a tour de force.

Wilbur Joseph Cash, son of Nannie Hamrick and John William Cash, was born in 1900 in Gaffney, South Carolina, but grew up in Boiling Springs, North Carolina, where his father was manager of a hosiery mill. A favorite haunt of young Cash was the excellent library of the local academy he attended. In 1922 he received a bachelor of arts degree from Wake Forest College, and he remained there for a year in the law school. He was a member of Dr. C. C. Pearson's very select political science club, an associate editor of the campus newspaper, *Old Gold and Black*, and a contributor to the college magazine, *Wake Forest Student*.

All the while a concept was evolving for his book about the South. Endless conversations with college friends helped Cash to crystallize his own ideas; impressions of life in a mill village led to a lasting hatred of injustice and hypocrisy; and the development of a thyroid abnormality made the author even more sensitive and obsessed with his introspective analyzing of the South. H. L. Mencken's "Sahara of the Bozart" struck a responsive chord in Cash, who emulated Mencken's style in several published articles of his own.

After teaching for two years, Cash became a journalist, writing intermittently as a freelancer and as a bona fide staff member of the *Charlotte News*.

Publication of *The Mind of the South* in February, 1941, earned for its author a Guggenheim Foundation Fellowship and acclaim from the literary world. However, he was exhausted, physically debilitated, and mentally disoriented. The brilliant writer committed suicide in Mexico City, where he had taken his bride and intended to write a novel. His tragic death ensured that Cash's reputation would rest on one remarkable book.

JOHN HARDEN

arrived in Raleigh in 1945 to be private secretary to Governor R. Gregg Cherry. For some time he had been collecting tales about North Carolina from newspapers, magazines, and live storytellers. He thought other Tar Heels would be as interested in them as he was, and soon he was narrating them over a weekly radio program. The response was immediate, and listeners sent him other yarns for his collection. Demand arose that they be preserved in a book. Thus it was that *The Devil's Tramping Ground and Other North Carolina Mystery Stories* appeared in 1949. The twenty short pieces told about ghost ships and the Brown Mountain Lights, about Peter Dromgoole, Theodosia Burr, and Peter Stuart Ney, about the rediscovery of the rare plant *Shortia galacifolia,* about "The Missing Major" and "The Mysterious Death of Beautiful Nell Cropsey." It was a rich harvest of the strange and curious.

Then, in 1954, he published *Tar Heel Ghosts,* thirty-three of the best stories from a whole filing cabinet of such tales in his writing studio. Within the book are "gentle ghosts and roistering ghosts; delicate lady ghosts and fishwife ghosts; homesick ghosts and ghosts that just want to be noticed"; and there are "small black crosses, galloping white horses, strangely moving lights, floating veils, lifelike apparitions, skulls, dripping blood, and 'things that go bump in the night.' "

Born in Graham in 1903, Harden attended local schools and then was graduated from the University of North Carolina at Chapel Hill. For twenty-one years he was a thoroughgoing newspaperman in Burlington, Raleigh, Charlotte, Salisbury, and Greensboro. In the 1940s he was active on the state's political scene and was affiliated with prominent state leaders. Since then he has served on numerous important boards and committees. Turning to industry in the 1950s Harden has built a successful career in the field of public relations.

Emerywood Studios

He has worked with civic, educational, and industrial concerns, including Burlington Mills and Cannon Mills. Since 1958 he has been the prime mover of his own firm, John Harden Associates. These varied experiences are reflected in his publications: *Alamance County: Economic and Social* (1928); *N.C. Highways and Their Builders* (1966); *Cannon* (forthcoming, 1981). He and his wife, Sarah Plexico Harden, live in Greensboro.

30

MANLY WADE WELLMAN

lives in Chapel Hill. From all appearances, though he follows one of the busiest schedules of any author in North Carolina, he is a completely calm and undisturbed man. He can write several books at the same time, be doing research on another, and throw off articles for newspapers and magazines in spare moments. Among his more-than-seventy books are science fiction, popular history, biography, novels, plays, and county history. Playing a guitar and teaching creative writing are also on his schedule.

His arrival in Chapel Hill came in a roundabout way. Born in 1903 in an interior province of Portuguese West Africa where his father was an American medical officer, young Wellman came to the United States at age six. After schooling in Washington, D.C., and Salt Lake City, he attended the University of Wichita in Kansas and then Columbia in New York. During newspaper jobs in Kansas, he began writing for the "pulps." In 1935 he headed for New York and started pouring out three or four thousand words a day for the magazines. Later, in the same year that his first book was published—a detective story, *Find My Killer* (1947)—he visited his father at Pinebluff, Moore County. He and his family decided to live there. In 1951 he moved to Chapel Hill to be close to the university library, where he can usually be found "researching" in the stacks. There he found material for *Dead and Gone* (1954), containing ten true, interesting North Carolina murders, and *Who Fears the Devil?* (1963), eleven frightening tales based on North Carolina folklore. *Worse Things Waiting* (1973) collects twenty-eight bizarre stories.

As a writer of adventure stories for boys, ages ten to fourteen, he is "tops." Four of them are set in Revolutionary North Carolina: *Rifles at Ramsour's Mill* (1961), *Battle for King's Mountain* (1962), *Clash on the Catawba* (1962), and *The South Fork Rangers* (1963). *Settlement on Shocco* (1963), winner of the Carolina Charter Tercentenary Commission literary competition, is about home-steaders in colonial Carolina. Exciting stories of the North Carolina mountains for the ten-to-fourteen age group are *The Master of Scare Hollow* (1964), *Mystery of Bear Paw Gap* (1965), *The Specter of Bear Paw Gap* (1966), and *Battle at Bear Paw Gap* (1966). Later publications include *The Kingdom of Madison* (1973), a county history, and *The Beyonders* (1977), science fiction. In 1978 he won the North Carolina Award.

F. ROY JOHNSON

Lawrence Wofford

is a complete book man who likes it that way. He is a historian of his eastern North Carolina, a one-man folklore society, and a recorder of old-time manners and customs. He belongs to the nineteenth century but is happily alive in the twentieth. Johnson publishes his own books as well as other people's—if they are in the general range of his interests—and occasionally reissues an out-of-print classic like John Brickell's *Natural History of North Carolina*, first published in 1737.

The writer-publisher was born in Bladen County on November 12, 1911, the son of John Fletcher and Minnie Caroline Henry Johnson. The elder Johnson, a farmer, also operated a steamboat on the Black River. Frank Roy attended local schools and was graduated in 1932 from Duke University with a B.A. degree. He was assistant editor of the Duke *Chronicle* and worked part-time as a commercial typist. In 1932 Johnson and his bride, Margaret Elizabeth Hamlin, went to live in Surry County, Virginia, on a farm owned by the bride's father, C. T. Hamlin. When Mr. Hamlin acquired a small hand-fed press powered by a foot pedal, Johnson became a printer, beginning with newspapers. From 1962 to 1980 he produced more than twenty books he wrote himself or in collaboration with others.

Five Indian books include *The Tuscaroras*, in two volumes (1967, 1968); *The Algonquins*, in two volumes (1972); and *Stories of the Old Cherokees* (1975). Seven books which explore various aspects of northeastern North Carolina social history are *The Peanut Story* (1964); *Tales from Old Carolina* (1965); *Before the Rebel Flag Fell* (1965), with collaborators Thomas C. Parramore and E. Frank Stephenson, Jr.; *The Nat Turner Slave Insurrection* (1966), with Thomas R. Gray's "The Confession, Trial and Execution of Nat Turner" as a supplement; *The Nat Turner Story* (1970); *Riverboating down Carolina Way* (1977); *The Gatling Gun and Flying Machine of Richard and Henry Gatling* (1979), with the collaboration of E. Frank Stephenson, Jr.

Books of legends and folklore, the "core" of Johnson's work, include *Witches and Demons in History and Folklore* (1971), *How and Why Stories in Carolina Folklore* (1971), *Supernaturals among Carolina Folk and Their Neighbors* (1977), and *Tales of Country Folks down Carolina Way* (1978).

32

RICHARD CHASE

is a nationally known folklorist who returned to
North Carolina in 1977 after a decade spent in
California. He is also entertainer, lecturer, and
author. And he lives right in the folklore
country—in the mountain community of Beech
Creek in Watauga County. Many of his folk
tales are collected there, he says. "And over in
Boone, the county seat, all summer long we
have folk festivals on a Saturday from about
three o'clock, and then we play games, sing
together, do country dances, listen to tales, and

Palmer's Photo Shop

hear banjos and fiddles and dulcimers. We have a lot of fun with the
Old Ways—the cultural heritage of our mountains—in all its living
uses with lively people." Often he is traveling far and wide in the Ap-
palachians, from Kentucky to Georgia, making talks, visiting schools,
and collecting new material. Richard Chase is a very busy man.

He was born near Huntsville, Alabama, in 1904. At twelve, he went
off to preparatory school at Bell Buckle, Tennessee, and studied Latin
and Greek along with the usual subjects. In college he majored in
botany. None of this was related to what has become his lifework. At
Pine Mountain Settlement School in the Kentucky Cumberland
mountains, he heard his first ballad. "After that chance visit," he
says, "everywhere I went, something relating to our heritage of
English-American ballads, songs, folk-hymns, tales, singing games,
country dances, seemed to take hold of me." It was natural that he
settle in the North Carolina mountains, where so much of America's
folk heritage is still unrecorded.

In 1933 as field representative of the Institute of Folk Music of the
University of North Carolina, Richard Chase began the special work
of teaching traditional songs and dances. *Old Songs and Singing
Games* (1938) was followed by *The Jack Tales* (1943) and *Grandfather
Tales* (1948), both of them a retelling of classic yarns—but with a
mountain flavor. After *Hullabaloo and Other Singing Folk Games*
(1949) came *Jack and the Three Sillies* (1950) and *Wicked John and
the Devil* (1951), single-tale picturebooks. More recent books by this
folklorist are *The Complete Tales of Uncle Remus* (1955), his excellent
collection *American Folk Tales and Songs* (1956), and *Billy Boy*
(1966).

JAMES STREET

once said that among his loves were boys and dogs (he had two sons and a daughter, by the way), and so it is not surprising that two of his many books are about them: *The Biscuit Eater* (1941) and *Good-bye, My Lady* (1954). After his death, his friend, the novelist Don Tracy, worked up James Street stories to make two other books: *Captain Little Ax* (1956), about a sixteen-year-old boy in the Confederate army, and *Pride of Possession* (1960), a tale of a boy hunting wild boar in the Great Smoky Mountains.

James Howell Street was born in Lumberton, Mississippi, October 15, 1903, and was educated in public school at nearby Laurel, Massey School in Pulaski, Tennessee, Southwestern Theological School, and Howard College. He began to write for local newspapers at age fifteen and married his childhood sweetheart at nineteen. Despite his Catholic upbringing, Street was a Baptist preacher for three years. From 1923 to 1937, he worked as a journalist, first in the South, then in the North. He left this second career to devote his full time to writing and was already famous when he moved to Chapel Hill in 1945 at the suggestion of William Meade Prince, an artist who had illustrated some of Street's stories about the Civil War for *Collier's* magazine. Quickly this fiery but personable man, small in stature, made himself a part of the town. He was, as he termed himself, "a professional writer"—a trained storyteller who had learned how to make a good living at the game. For instance, a short story published in 1937, "A Letter to the World," was made into the motion picture *Nothing Sacred*, which in turn became the Broadway musical comedy *Hazel Flagg*. James Street once said he had written more stories and articles than he could remember.

Look Away (1936), *Oh, Promised Land* (1940), and *Tap Roots* (1942) are among his best-known titles, leading up to his greatest popular success, *The Gauntlet* (1945), the story of a Baptist preacher,

published the year he moved to North Carolina. *The High Calling* (1951) is a sequel. Many readers think his best novel is *The Velvet Doublet* (1953), a story of Columbus's times. *The Civil War* (1953) and *The Revolutionary War* (1954) irreverently shatter favorite American myths. *James Street's South* (1955) was published after his death on September 28, 1954.

GLENN TUCKER

was a three-time Mayflower Cup winner who retired from the business world in 1948, bought an apple farm called "Filibuster Hall" in the Upward community near Flat Rock in the mountains of Henderson County, planted more apple trees, then sat down to do the thing he had been dreaming about for years: write books. True, he had managed to publish two books before then, in 1937 and 1945, but the kind he now had in mind demanded more than weekends and evening hours. While the apples were growing, he wanted long, long days for indefatigable research into the facts, facts, facts—for Glenn Tucker was a biographer and historian who believed that only facts, not theories, are dependable.

He was born on November 30, 1892, in Tampico, Indiana, the son of a physician. He made a brilliant record at DePauw University and the Columbia School of Journalism. After newspaper jobs in the Midwest and a stint with the army in France during World War I, he became White House correspondent for the *New York World*. For twenty-one years beginning in 1927, he was a member of public-relations and advertising firms in Philadelphia and New York. Then came the break and the opportunity to write more.

At his mountain home near Fairview, North Carolina, to which he moved in 1966 when he gave up apple growing, he rose before dawn to get to his desk. In the tranquillity of early morning, ideas and words came readily. Often, with the help of his wife Dorothy, he was away in some distant city, digging for facts among the records. Among his books are two winners of the Mayflower Cup. *Poltroons and Patriots* (2 volumes, 1954) is a popular history of the War of 1812; *Tecumseh* (1956) details the life of the famous Indian leader; and *Dawn Like Thunder* (1963) concerns the Barbary pirates of North Africa and the birth of the United States Navy. When the Civil War centennial approached, he turned his attention to that period and wrote several notable books: *High Tide at Gettysburg* (1958); *Hancock the Superb* (1960), about a neglected Federal general; *Chickamauga* (1961); *Front Rank: The Story of North Carolina in the Civil War* (1963); *Zeb Vance: Champion of Personal Freedom* (1965); and *Lee and Longstreet at Gettysburg* (1968). Later works were *The War of 1812* (1969) and *Mad Anthony Wayne and the New Nation* (1973).

Barber, Hendersonville

35

HARRY GOLDEN

first came to North Carolina in 1939, was convinced he wanted to live here, and in 1941, as he says, "I landed in Charlotte with only a cigar and a prayer." He founded the *Carolina Israelite*, a monthly newspaper for which he wrote all the material, some 20,000 words an issue. It quickly caught on, with its discussions of racial and religious minorities, its observations on anything and everything, mostly witty. His comments did not fail to stir controversy,

Tom Carroll   on which Golden thrived.

Then came the crucial year 1958. First his office-residence in Charlotte was destroyed by fire. A few months afterward *Only in America* was published and hit the best-seller lists. The book, edited by his son, with a preface by Carl Sandburg, was made up of 184 pieces from the *Israelite*. Later it was made into a Broadway play and sold over a million copies in a paperback edition. In September, a painful period from his past, involving financial matters, made national headlines. Undaunted, the resilient Golden began a syndicated newspaper column and traveled the world to make speeches. The *Israelite* ceased publication in 1968.

Harry Golden was born on the lower East Side of New York City, May 6, 1902; his father was an Austrian immigrant. He attended high school at night and memorized all of Julius Caesar's speeches from the Shakespeare play before he was eighteen. After graduation from City College of New York, he worked on newspapers, then entered a brokerage firm with disastrous results. On one of a number of subsequent jobs, he came to North Carolina. Now divorced, Harry Golden is the father of three grown sons.

A pamphlet, *Jewish Roots in the Carolinas* (1955), preceded *Only in America* (1958), which was closely followed by two similar books, *For 2¢ Plain* (1959) and *Enjoy, Enjoy* (1960). In *Carl Sandburg* (1961), Golden wrote an informal biography of his close friend. Among his other books are: *You're Entitle'* (1962), essays; *Forgotten Pioneer* (1963), about the American pack peddler before the days of paved highways; *The Right Time* (1968), an autobiography; *The Israelis* (1970); *The Golden Book of Jewish Humor* (1971); *Travels through Jewish America* (1973); *Our Southern Landsmen* (1974); and *Long Live Columbus* (1975). He won the North Carolina Award in 1979.

BETTY SMITH

was, of course, the author of *A Tree Grows in Brooklyn* (1943), reputed to be one of the ten best-selling books of all time. The result of three years' work, the novel was loosely based on the author's girlhood in that famous borough of New York City. More than four million copies have been printed, it has been translated into sixteen languages, and both a motion picture and a Broadway musical show were based on it. Certainly the book made the author wealthy.

Thomas P. Inman

Betty (Keogh) Smith was born of Irish and German parents in Brooklyn, December 15, 1904. She stopped public school after the eighth grade, left Brooklyn at the age of seventeen, then was married at eighteen to a law student attending the University of Michigan at Ann Arbor. She was herself a special student at the university, and later at Yale for courses in the drama. In 1936, on the invitation of Paul Green and "Proff" Koch, she came to Chapel Hill and received a grant in playwriting from the Rockefeller Foundation. In the midst of keeping house, writing plays, and seeing two daughters through school, she started writing *A Tree Grows in Brooklyn*. Though the success of this book and later ones might have impelled her to leave the village of Chapel Hill, she restored the "old Mangum house" on Rosemary Street, and there she lived with "Misty," a white cat, and "No-Name," a shaggy sheepdog. Periodically she conducted courses in creative writing at the university.

In addition to being the author of four novels, she compiled several anthologies of drama and wrote, generally in collaboration with others, more than a hundred plays for amateur production. Twenty of them are about North Carolina. Her most frequent collaborator was the playwright Robert Finch, her third husband, who died in 1959.

Her second novel, *Tomorrow Will Be Better* (1948), was, like the first, about family life in Brooklyn. *Maggie-Now* (1958), treating Brooklyn of an earlier period, won the Sir Walter Raleigh Award. *Joy in the Morning* (1963) is semiautobiographical in that it deals with the marriage of a young couple in a midwestern university. She died in Shelton, Connecticut, on January 17, 1972, before she was able to complete a novel with a Chapel Hill setting.

GLEN ROUNDS

was born on a ranch in the Bad Lands of South Dakota in 1906 and grew up there and in Montana. He studied painting and drawing at the Art Institute in Kansas City and the Art Students' League in New York. His subjects were the cowboys and lumberjacks he had known as a boy. From time to time, Rounds has been known as muleskinner, medicine man, lightning artist, hobo, rodeo rider, sign painter, artillerist, textile designer, naturalist, cowboy, and carnival man. He is a good storyteller too, and in New York was advised by some friends to write up what he talked about. His first book came in 1936, and since then, he says, "I've combined painting, writing and illustrating. My writing is never quite separated from my pictures; often they progress side by side." All of his books are juveniles, all of them using his own art work, though he often illustrates books written by others. He visited North Carolina in 1937, married Margaret Umstead of Sanford a year later, but did not settle permanently at Pinebluff till 1945, after a tour of duty in World War II. He has one son.

Glen Rounds has written an impressive number of books. The first ones, naturally, dealt with the people and animals on the plains of the West. *Whitey's First Roundup* (1942) created a pint-size cowboy whose adventures have been recorded in many sequels. In the mid-1950s, the North Carolina scene began to creep into his stories. *Swamp Life* (1957), a very popular book about the Sandhills, dealt, according to Rounds, "with raccoons, hell divers, wood ducks and others who live in the hollow trees, tangled thickets and swampy places along Little Fiery Creek—with a few words of advice on how to see and become acquainted with them." A companion volume, *Wildlife at Your Doorstep* (1958), took up insects, reptiles, and small woods animals. *Wild Orphan* (1961) tells of a young beaver who must get along by himself. *Rain in the Woods and Other Small Matters* (1964) deals with those wild creatures, including the otter and tent cater-

Holiday House Publishers

pillar, inhabiting Rounds's own pond and woods and tells what they do when it rains. Three times Rounds has won the AAUW Award for the best book of the year for juveniles: in 1961, with *Beaver Business: An Almanac*; in 1967, with *The Snake Tree*; and in 1976, with *Mr. Yowder and the Lion Roar Capsules*. Still another book about beavers came in 1976, *The Beaver: How He Works*.

ALEXANDER KEY

writes science fiction which appeals especially to boys. Named for his father, the novelist was born in La Plata, Maryland, September 21, 1904, son of Charlotte Ryder and Alexander Hill Key, Sr. Aspiring to be a painter and illustrator as well as a free-lance writer, Key attended the Chicago Art Institute for two years, 1921-1923, and later taught at the institute. In 1929 he became seriously interested in writing for juveniles. *Red Eagle* was published in 1930, with *Liberty or Death* coming out in 1931. In 1941 he wrote *Caroliny Trail*, which has its setting in North Carolina, his adopted state. During 1942-1945 Key served in the United States Navy, attaining the rank of lieutenant commander. After returning to civilian life, the author wrote an adult novel, *The Wrath and the Wind* (1949), and had many articles and works of fiction published in magazines, including the *Saturday Evening Post* and *Cosmopolitan.*

Since the 1960s Key has concentrated on writing books for young people, frequently using a setting reminiscent of the mountain area around Franklin, North Carolina, where the family lives—Key, his wife Alice Towle Key, and their child Zan. Science fiction has become his forte and three books of this genre have won the AAUW Award. *The Forgotten Key* (1965) tells of Jon, a boy who fell from another planet to a place on earth much like western North Carolina. When earthlings try to exploit Jon's special gift of mind reading, he becomes disillusioned by the complex, mechanized life on this planet. *Escape to Witch Mountain* (1968) is another story of strange children with unusual powers; it was later produced as a Walt Disney movie. *The Magic Meadow* (1975) is a fantasy in which Brick, a young boy who is incurably ill, learns how to "teleport" himself and his friends to a lovely secret place far beyond the confines of Ward Nine in Belleview Hospital.

Return from Witch Mountain, made in 1978 into a successful Walt Disney movie, tells how Tia and Tony, young

Westminster Press

space people from another planet, visit earth and encounter an unscrupulous doctor who wants to exploit Tony's special powers. Other science fiction books by Key include *Rivets and Sprockets* (1964), a story about a little robot; *Bolts: A Robot dog* (1966); *The Incredible Tide* (1970); and *Flight to the Lonesome Place* (1971).

KERMIT HUNTER

Bernadette Hoyle

once wrote about his literary convictions: "I share with Paul Green the idea that the outdoor drama represents the greatest challenge today, in that out of the urge of local areas for expression can come a new era in American drama." To meet the challenge, he started out with *Unto These Hills* (1950), the Indian "symphonic drama" which, given annually at Cherokee, has been seen by over a million spectators. *Horn in the West* (since 1952), telling the story of Daniel Boone and the Southern Appalachian frontier, is produced in the Watauga County town of Boone near the Blue Ridge Parkway. Hunter has fashioned other dramas for historical occasions in Illinois, Arizona, Florida, Tennessee, Pennsylvania, Kentucky, Virginia, West Virginia, and South Carolina. Thus the formula which Paul Green "invented" has been generously employed and expanded by his pupil. By 1966 he had completed his twenty-sixth outdoor drama.

Kermit Hunter came to North Carolina in 1947. Born in 1910 in the coal-mining country of southern West Virginia, he began writing at an early age. Music, too, attracted him. After undergraduate days at Ohio State University, where poetry was his principal interest, he later went to Juilliard School of Music in New York. During the 1930s he was variously a newspaperman, chamber of commerce secretary, baseball team manager, organist, and choir director. After war service as an army officer, he went to Chapel Hill to study drama. From then on, writing became a major activity. *Unto These Hills* was his master's thesis at the University of North Carolina at Chapel Hill in 1949. Its immediate success prompted him to stay on in the state. He taught English at Chapel Hill, was married, and in 1965 earned a Ph.D. degree. After a year as a Guggenheim Fellow, he accepted a position in the Department of English at Hollins College, Virginia. In 1964 he went to Southern Methodist University in Texas as dean of the School of Arts. He retired in 1976.

Outdoor drama represents only one aspect of his writing. Both one-act and full-length plays for the indoor theater have been produced. *The Third Frontier* helped New Bern celebrate her two-hundred-and-fiftieth birthday in 1960. Hunter still composes most of the music for his shows. He feels that success in literature is measured by one's "idealism and integrity."

THAD STEM, JR.

was a poet and essayist born in Oxford, January 24, 1916. At Oxford High School, Darlington School in Georgia, and Duke University, he participated in football, basketball, and, he says, "just went to school." Back in Oxford, he tried his hand with short stories and sketches, but there was no poetry. After service in World War II, he returned home and became Granville County's Veterans Service Officer. In 1947 he married the portrait painter Marguerite Anderson. After his venture into poetry about 1944—

J. B. Clay

from the first, a poetry of metaphor and simile—he commented that all his writing was "predicated upon an interpretation of rural and small-town manners and customs" and that his prose was "largely descriptive and lyrical."

Frequently he contributed feature stories to the state newspapers on history and the ways of olden times. His unsigned, but easily recognized, editorials in the Raleigh *News and Observer* were widely copied.

His first two books were *Picture Poems* (1949), then *The Jackknife Horse* (1954), which was the winner of the Roanoke-Chowan Award for the year's best book of poetry by a North Carolinian. The next two, *The Perennial Almanac* (1959) and *The Animal Fair* (1960), established him as a writer of the short lyric essay. *Penny Whistles and Wild Plums* (1962) offers an unusual combination of twenty-eight poems with prose commentary; *Spur Line* (1966) also combines poems and prose commentary. *Light and Rest* (1964) tells, in short prose pieces, what it felt like to grow up in a small southern town several decades ago. After the essays in *A Flagstone Walk* (1968) and the poems in *Journey Proud* (1970) came *Entries from Oxford* (1971), a "profane" history of his home town, and *The Tar Heel Press* (1973), a narrative of North Carolina newspapers. *Thad Stem's First Reader* was published in 1976 and *Ransacking Words and Customs from A to Izzard* in 1977. Thaddeus Garland Stem, Jr., died June 22, 1980.

has been admired by both critics and readers from the time her first short story appeared. It is a happy situation in which to find oneself. Frequently, a book sells widely but is roasted by the reviewers; again, the critics praise a volume but the paying customers stay away. Mrs. Patton has attracted both groups, and understandably so. Her style is polished to the last word, her characters are urbane but very human, and the reviewers are all respectful. On the other hand, her plots are clever, her situations recognizable to the average reader, and the public approves. Thus Mrs. Patton is the picture itself of a successful author.

Always, she says, she had done a bit of writing, but her career came later than most. She was born in Raleigh in 1906, her father a newspaperman. "Newspapermen in those days were almost as nomadic as Methodist ministers," she explains; and she lived in various towns in the Carolinas and Virginia, though Raleigh was always *home.* "At sixteen I entered Trinity College in Durham but transferred the next year to Chapel Hill." There she wrote plays for Professor Koch of the Carolina Playmakers. She continues: "I never received a degree, as mathematics was beyond me; and I retired, voluntarily, from college about six weeks before I was supposed to graduate and have never attended a class of any kind since then." At twenty-one she was married to Dr. Lewis Patton of the Department of English at Duke. They have twin daughters and a son, all now married. For the University of North Carolina at Chapel Hill and at Greensboro, she has taught classes in creative writing.

After the short plays of the Chapel Hill days, she laid her pen aside. Not till the children were along in school did she, at her husband's suggestion, start again. Soon her stories appeared regularly in the *New Yorker,* which has published most of her work, as well as in *Harper's, Collier's,* and other well-known journals. These stories have

been collected in *The Finer Things of Life* (1951) and *A Piece of Luck* (1955). The novel *Good Morning, Miss Dove* (1954), a Book-of-the-Month-Club selection, was made into a motion picture. All three books won the Sir Walter Raleigh Award for outstanding fiction by a North Carolinian. In 1966 North Carolina State University presented to her an honorary degree, and in 1970 she won the North Carolina Award.

OVID WILLIAMS PIERCE

has roots which go deep into the soil of northeastern North Carolina. His forefathers came from nearby Virginia into Halifax County in 1812, bought large holdings there, and moved in an aristocratic society of plantation owners. Such was the heritage of Ovid Williams Pierce, born October 1, 1910, in Weldon. From the schools there, he went to Duke University, where he developed a literary interest as editor of the *Archive*, undergraduate literary journal. After graduation he helped his father in the operation of the spacious farms and a peanut plant in Halifax County, then went to Harvard for a master's degree in English. In World War II, he was a counterintelligence army officer with various posts in the Caribbean. For ten years after the war he taught in English departments at Southern Methodist University in Texas and at Tulane University in Louisiana, then in 1956 came back to North Carolina to join the faculty at East Carolina College. There was a pressing need for the change of jobs, for during the several previous years Pierce had been rebuilding an old farmhouse fifteen miles from Weldon on a 350-acre tract he had inherited. This beautiful two-storied mansion is where Pierce, now retired from teaching, writes at leisure and where in bachelor fashion he entertains his friends.

Two novels have won the Sir Walter Raleigh Award for outstanding fiction by a North Carolinian. *The Plantation* (1953) is the story of rural life in postbellum North Carolina. In it, a gentle-hearted plantation owner gives up career and love in order to provide for his spinster sisters and to keep the homeplace intact. Excited critics lavished ecstatic praise on Pierce for his distinguished prose and for his avoidance of the stereotypes implicit in the moonlight-and-magnolias school of southern fiction. *On a Lonesome Porch* (1960), with a similar setting, works out a new life for the remaining members of a plantation aristocracy at the end of the Civil War. A third novel was *The Wedding Guest* (1974).

The apprenticeship springboard to these novels was the writing of numerous short stories, some of which appeared in the 1930s. His poetic article "North Carolina," written for *Holiday* magazine, was included in *American Panorama* (1961). Winner of the North Carolina Award in 1969, Pierce in 1976 published a collection of short works, *Old Man's Gold and Other Stories.*

43

JULIA MONTGOMERY STREET

wrote the best book for young people by a North Carolinian in 1955-1956, its title *Fiddler's Fancy*. For this volume she received the American Association of University Women Award. Surprisingly enough, it was her first juvenile work. *Fiddler's Fancy*, for ages nine to twelve, is about the mountain folk of the Toe River region of Mitchell County. The time is about 1875. The prototype for the heroine, Angeline, was an actual woman known by the novelist and was in her nineties when the book came out. All except the plot of *Fiddler's Fancy* is true—the mountain speech, folklore, and customs, even the setting, which is a farm near Bakersville where the author's husband grew up. *Moccasin Tracks* (1958) is a story of the Cherokee and the boyhood of Timothy Martin (the fictional name for William Holland Thomas) who later became their "Great White Chief." *Candle Love Feast* (1959), for ages five to nine, is about the Moravian Christmas. *Drover's Gold* (1961), for boys ten to fourteen, tells of a young fellow's adventures when he runs away from home to join drovers of six hundred hogs to market down the Buncombe Turnpike before the coming of the railroads. *Dulcie's Whale* (1963), a story about Cape Lookout in 1918 for ages eight to twelve, brought Mrs. Street the American Association of University Women Award for the second time. *North Carolina Parade* (1966), written in collaboration with Richard Walser and winner of the 1966 AAUW Award, has stories from history and biography told in such a way that the young reader will sense the greatness of his North Carolina heritage.

Mrs. Street is a Tar Heel all the way. She was born January 19, 1898, in Concord, grew up in Apex and Raleigh, went to the University of North Carolina at Greensboro, taught grammar grades, traveled for the Children's Home Society, and now lives in Winston-Salem. Her husband, now deceased, was a Winston-Salem pediatrician. Not too far away are a son and a daughter and a number of grandchildren. She paints landscapes now and then, can weave a swatch of cloth, or play folk songs on her mountain dulcimer. Before *Fiddler's Fancy*, she published two little books of poetry: *Street Lights* (1949) and *Salem Christmas Eve* (1956), both in small editions now unavailable. In 1975 she published *Judaculla's Handprint and Mysterious Tales from North Carolina*.

PEGGY HOFFMANN

published her first book when her daughter
Rosemary Birky was seven years old. It all came
about when Rosemary was taking lessons in the
kitchen arts from her mother, who decided to
write up some of the things that went on. It was
called *Miss B's First Cookbook* (1950) and in a
decade sold over 30,000 copies. The lessons continued, and so did the books. *Sew Easy!* (1956),
published when Rosemary was thirteen, is full
of diagrams, sketches, and photographs; the
text describes in simple words just how to go
about those first days with a needle and thread. A sequel, *Sew Far,
Sew Good!* (1958), for ages fourteen and up, suggests plans for a girl's
wardrobe. Rosemary's two brothers, Teddy and Bruce, finally got a
break in their mother's writing career with *The Wild Rocket* (1960)
and *Shift to High!* (1965), both novels for older boys. In the first, a
fifteen-year-old lad sets off a homemade rocket; and in the second,
three friends have some amusing adventures on a motor camping
trip. *A Forest of Feathers* (1965) is an adult novel inspired by the
writer's experiences as a music therapist at Butner Mental Hospital.
Maryland during the time of the War of 1812 is the setting for the
novel *My Dear Cousin* (1970). Two collections of stories are *The
Money Hat* (1969), Hungarian folk tales, and *The Sea Wedding* (1978),
folk tales from Estonia. She collaborated with Frank Watson in
writing *Been There and Back* (1977).

Mrs. Hoffmann, born in Delaware, Ohio, worked her way through
Miami University in that state, doing everything from baby-sitting to
tutoring in Spanish. After a year of graduate study at the University
of Chicago, she married Arnold E. Hoffmann in 1935. They returned
to Ohio after a stay in Florida, and there Dr. Hoffmann became a
professor of music. As a faculty wife, Mrs. Hoffmann attended a cir-
cle of those interested in creative writing. She complied with the re-
quirement to submit written material and "stand up to criticism";
two years later she sold her first article for $12. In 1950 Dr.
Hoffmann became state supervisor of music in the North Carolina
public schools. Since moving to Raleigh, Mrs. Hoffmann, has been a
church organist and has issued several books—all collections and
arrangements—for church choirs. She is active in the poetry-for-
public-schools program.

ROBERT RUARK

lived a life which was the very symbol of excitement and success. Born in Wilmington, December 29, 1915, he grew up there, spending ample time with his grandfather down the Cape Fear River at Southport. He graduated in journalism at the university at Chapel Hill, kept a newspaper job briefly at Hamlet, then went to sea as a merchant seaman. Later in Washington, D.C., he moved from copy boy at the *Star* to the sports department of the *Daily News*. There he hit his stride. In 1938 he was married. After duty in the Atlantic and Pacific as a naval officer in World War II, he returned to Washington and made his syndicated column a $40,000-a-year job by unmasking such sacred institutions as southern cooking, American women, and army generals. In travels around the world seeking copy for his columns, he turned up in Africa and went on safari in the jungle. In the mid-1950s he settled permanently in Spain, but without a letup in his columns, articles, and books. He died in London, July 1, 1965, and is buried at Palamos, north of Barcelona.

Robert Ruark once said that "the best writing I will ever do" was in his book of childhood reminiscences, *The Old Man and the Boy* (1957), a series of pieces set in and around Southport in which a boy (Ruark himself) is guided tenderly and wisely by his grandfather in the art of hunting, fishing, and training dogs. *The Old Man's Boy Grows Older* (1961) is a sequel.

Ruark's twelve books fall conveniently into pairs. His first book was *Grenadine Etching* (1947), a narrative burlesque spoofing the historical novel, its sequel *Grenadine's Spawn* (1952) pursuing the alarming careers of Grenadine's children. The spiciest material from his newspaper column made up *I Didn't Know It Was Loaded* (1948) and *One for the Road* (1949). *Horn of the Hunter* (1953) and *Use Enough Gun* (1966) are accounts of hunting big game in East Africa. *Something of Value* (1955), and *Uhuru* (1962) are successful novels of

Gene Hyde Associates

violence in Africa. Two other novels are *Poor No More* (1959), the story of a North Carolina boy who became a ruthless business tycoon, and *The Honey Badger* (1965), about the spiritual poverty of a middle-aged writer who has roamed three continents.

46

BURKE DAVIS

was born in Durham on July 24, 1913, but when he was only six, the family moved to Greensboro. While he was in high school, his mother prodded him into submitting a paper in a contest. He won the prize. As he recalls it, the title of his winning essay was "My Experiences as a Snake Man in the Boy Scouts." At Guilford and Duke and the university at Greensboro, he haphazardly studied for a career in advertising; but later he ambled into journalism and accepted newspaper jobs in Charlotte, Baltimore, and finally back in Greensboro. In 1960 he left Greensboro and from 1960 to 1980 served as special projects writer for Colonial Williamsburg, Inc. The North Carolina Award was presented to him in 1973 by Governor James E. Holshouser, Jr.

His first book for young readers was *Roberta E. Lee* (1956), about a Chatham County rabbit who was an honest-to-goodness southern belle. Two histories for students are *America's First Army* (1962), on the colonial militia, and *Appomattox* (1963). Also for young readers is *Rebel Raider: A Biography of Admiral Semmes* (1966), about a Confederate hero, coauthored by Evangeline Davis; *Heroes of the American Revolution* (1971); *Biography of a Leaf* (1973); *Biography of a King Snake* (1975); *Runaway Balloon: The Last Flight of the Confederate Air Force One* (1976); *Black Heroes of the American Revolution* (1976); *Biography of a Fish Hawk* (1977); *Mr. Lincoln's Whiskers* (1978).

Whisper My Name (1949) is a contemporary novel based on an incident he had learned about in Charlotte. *The Ragged Ones* (1951) and *Yorktown* (1952) are historical novels of Revolutionary times. In both, Davis employs a realistic, human treatment. Beginning with *They Called Him Stonewall* (1954), he turned to the Civil War period. His biography of Jackson was followed by *Gray Fox* (1956), the story of Lee's Civil War years, and *Jeb Stuart: The Last Cavalier* (1957). Two years after this, *To Appomattox: Nine April Days, 1865* (1959) won the Mayflower Cup. *Our Incredible Civil War* (1960) explores some previously hushed-up facts about our battling forefathers, but *The Cowpens-Guilford Courthouse Campaign* (1962) is straight history. He returned to fiction with *The Summer Land* (1965). Of several later Davis publications, *The Billy Mitchell Affair* (1967) and *Sherman's March* (1980) are outstanding.

Colonial Williamsburg

47

CARL SANDBURG

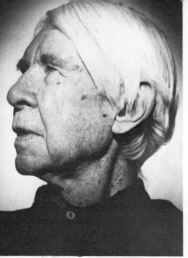

bought a 240-acre farm at Flat Rock, near Hendersonville, in 1945 and the following spring moved down from Michigan. The reason for the change of residence was *goats!* Ten years before this, Mrs. Sandburg had begun raising them to provide a small farm income from a Wisconsin property inadequate for cows. It was a business, not a hobby. After the move to Michigan, it was soon found out that the climate was not suitable for goat-raising. The Blue Ridge country was. Goats need hills and year-round pasturage. At beautiful Connemara, the old residence of the Confederate Secretary of the Treasury Christopher G. Memminger, specially designed barns were built, and the goats thrived. The herd of pedigreed Nubian and Tobbenburg goats soon were winning championships all over North and South America. But Connemara had other attractions. There, in a study on the top floor, America's great poet, novelist, and biographer could find quiet for his work. The house was large, with plenty of room for Sandburg's huge private library. For a folklorist and song collector like C. S., the North Carolina mountains yielded rich materials, as they have always done. There was always folk singing in the little communities nearby. The farm itself, at a 2,500-foot altitude and with a view of forty miles across the Blue Ridge, was a comfortable spot for the poet's visiting daughters and grandchildren, for the dogs and horses as well as the goats. And Carl Sandburg loved sitting on the steps of Connemara, singing and playing his guitar for children and family and visitors. His 21-year residence in North Carolina ended with his death at Connemara on July 22, 1967.

The events of the first sixty-seven years of Carl Sandburg's life are easily available elsewhere. Born in 1878 in Galesburg, Illinois, of Swedish immigrant parents, he received a haphazard education. Daylaborer, soldier, and newspaperman—he moved to poetry and became the "laureate of industrial America." This famed biographer of Lincoln, generally thought of as a midwesterner, was once asked if he was now a Tar Heel. "I pay taxes here," he said; "I write here; and I shall die here: indeed I *am* a North Carolina writer." He received the Roanoke-Chowan Poetry Award in 1960 and 1961. In 1974 Connemara, unchanged from the time of Sandburg's death, was opened to the public.

A. R. AMMONS

is a major American poet in the tradition of Ralph Waldo Emerson and Walt Whitman. Many of his poems, such as the often reprinted "Neely Myers," grew out of boyhood experiences in North Carolina; and his nature lyrics reflect strolls along the seashore, hikes in peaceful hills, or restful hours in his own backyard. However, Ammons sometimes uses unconventional themes and deviates boldly in style and form. He writes confidently and ingeniously of stockmarkets and football as well as of seas and forests.

Cornell University News Bureau

Archie Randolph Ammons, son of W. M. and Lucy McKee Ammons, was born in Columbus County, February 18, 1926, and attended the Whiteville public schools. After serving from 1944 to 1946 in the South Pacific with the United States Navy, he enrolled at Wake Forest College and received a B.S. degree in 1949, the same year that he married Phyllis Plumbo. The Ammonses have one son, John Randolph. After a year as principal of the Hatteras Elementary School, Ammons in 1950 entered the University of California at Berkeley, this time concentrating on English. From 1952 to 1961 he was executive vice-president of a business firm, Friedrich and Dimmock, Inc., Millville, New Jersey. During 1963 he was poetry editor of *Nation* (New York) and in 1964 joined the English faculty at Cornell University, where since 1973 he has been the Goldwyn Smith Professor of Humanities.

Ammons launched his literary career by financing publication of a few copies of *Ommateum* ["Compound Eye"], *with Doxology*. Now a copy of that first modest volume of verse is a prized collector's item! In 1965 came the unique *Tape for the Turn of the Year*, a journal in verse written on an adding machine. *Collected Poems 1951-1971* (1972) won the 1973 National Book Award for Poetry. Other publications include: *Expressions of Sea Level* (1964); *Corsons Inlet* (1965); *Northfield Poems* (1966); *Selected Poems* (1968); *Uplands* (1970); *Briefings: Poems Small and Easy* (1971); *Sphere: The Form of a Motion* (1974); *Diversifications* (1975); *The Snow Poems* (1977).

The poet's numerous honors include a Guggenheim Fellowship, 1966; a National Endowment for the Arts grant, 1969; the Oscar Young Award, 1968; the Levinson Poetry Award, 1970; the Bollingen Prize for 1973-1974; and selection as Faculty Fellow, Society for the Humanities, 1973-1974.

NELL WISE WECHTER

was born August 6, 1913, in the Dare County village of Stumpy Point on Pamlico Sound. For generations, her forebears had lived on the Outer Banks. Even today she speaks with the rich, full accent of the salt-water country. Her father, a fisherman whose considerable holdings were wiped out in the hurricane of 1930, praised her school compositions and encouraged her longing to be a writer. There was never much cash in the tiny isolated village. Mrs. Wechter says: "I sold papers in the village every afternoon after school to pay for my high school ring, my high school diploma, and all the other things I had to have. If I remember correctly, I cleared roughly about $3.00 a week." She was valedictorian of her high school class. Then she borrowed enough money to complete the two-year normal course at East Carolina Teachers College. In 1933 she signed up for grades 1 through 4 at a one-teacher school at Frisco on the Hatteras Banks. The day before she arrived, a hurricane blew the schoolhouse entirely away. After five years of teaching in Northampton County, she returned to Cape Hatteras for the next four years. There, during World War II (see *Taffy of Torpedo Junction*), she taught and lived in the dangerous area, and met her husband Robert Wechter, chief pharmacist's mate. After the war, the Wechters with their daughter moved inland and pursued their education at East Carolina and the University of North Carolina at Chapel Hill. Following a year in Lumberton, they moved in 1953 to Greensboro, where both taught in the public schools till their retirement.

An apprenticeship of newspaper writing, magazine articles, and prize essays culminated in *Taffy of Torpedo Junction* (1957), a Cape Hatteras story of World War II in which a girl with her dog and Banker pony solves a mystery involving German submarines. Written for ages ten to sixteen, this novel, which catches the spirit of the Sand Banks in a way impossible for one not born and bred there, won

the American Association of University Women Award as the best North Carolina juvenile book of the year. A second juvenile novel, *Besty Dowdy's Ride* (1960), deals with a Revolutionary legend. It was followed by *Swamp Girl* (1971), about Dare County today, and a Blackbeard novel, *Teach's Light* (1974). *Some Whisper of Our Name* (1975) is a later book about Dare County.

DAVID STICK

decided long ago that he would not be the kind of writer who ranged both near and far for his material. Instead, he staked his claim on one region, began to learn every little thing about it, and wrote his books only when his files and notebooks were jammed with information. His "stake" was the coastal area of North Carolina. First he wrote *Fabulous Dare* (1949), a brief county history. Then, in *Graveyard of the Atlantic* (1952), he published a major work, carefully documented and researched, concerning more than six hundred shipwrecks on the dangerous North Carolina coast. The book was highly praised and widely read. *The Outer Banks of North Carolina, 1584-1958* (1958) came after years of study—a fascinating history of the coastal country from the Virginia line to Beaufort Inlet. The last two books were illustrated by his father Frank Stick, artist and businessman. For the pictures in *The Cape Hatteras Seashore* (1964) David Stick supplied a poetic text.

David Stick's concentration on a single North Carolina region is somewhat surprising, since he is not native. He was born at Interlaken, New Jersey, December 21, 1919, but moved to Dare County in 1928. While a student at Elizabeth City High School, he wrote for the local papers. After a year at the University of North Carolina at Chapel Hill, he hitchhiked over the United States to gain experience. As a Marine Corps combat correspondent during World War II, he was present at Leyte and Okinawa. Two years of magazine work in New York followed; then in 1947 he went back "home" to Kitty Hawk. Though his real estate interests soon consumed most of his time, he managed to operate a bookstore for many years and to serve as president of the Nags Head Tourist Bureau, the Duck Woods Country Club, and Dare County Tourist Bureau, as well as to head up the Board of Directors of North Carolinians for Better Libraries. Interested in protecting the Sand Banks from overexploitation, Stick has been a promoter of the National Seashore Park. His *Dare County: A History* (1970) and *North Carolina Lighthouses* (1980) are small books which have been extremely popular.

FRANK G. SLAUGHTER

was a practicing surgeon when his first successful book was published. Five years later he became a professional writer, using his medical experience as background material. He has to his credit more than fifty titles, some under the pseudonym C. V. Terry.

Frank Gill Slaughter was born on February 25, 1908, in Washington, D.C., and now lives most of the year in Jacksonville, Florida, but he was reared and educated in North Carolina and has maintained ties with the state. His parents, Stephen Lucius and Sallie Nicholson Gill Slaughter, operated a tobacco farm near Berea and Oxford in Granville County. Young Frank, a brilliant student, entered Trinity College (now Duke University) when he was fourteen, was elected to Phi Beta Kappa, and in 1926 was graduated magna cum laude. Four years later he received an M.D. degree from Johns Hopkins Medical School and established himself as a surgeon in Jefferson Hospital in Roanoke, Virginia. In 1933 he married Jane Mundy, a Roanoke girl; the Slaughters have two sons. Dr. Slaughter served in the United States Army Medical Corps, 1942-1946, and rose to the rank of lieutenant colonel.

His writing for recreation led to the publishing of the book *That None Should Die*. Its 1941 publication in Denmark was an unprecedented success, and in it Slaughter perfected his formula for historical novels—a doctor or Biblical hero involved in a fast-moving plot; timely subject matter such as socialized medicine, tranquilizing drugs, organ transplants, wars; and fresh, imaginative use of the sin-suffer-repent pattern. Millions of Slaughter books in various translations have been sold around the world.

Two of the best of the doctor novels are set in North Carolina: *In a Dark Garden* (1940) and its sequel, *The Stubborn Heart* (1950). *Doctors' Wives*, a best-seller in 1967, was made into a popular motion picture. Especially for juveniles is *Apalachee Gold: The Fabulous Adventures of Cabeza de Vaca*, (1954). Fiction based on Biblical characters and events comprise much of the Slaughter canon—for example, *The Road to Bithynia* (1951) and *Upon This Rock* (1963). Books of nonfiction include *Medicine for Moderns: The New Science of Psychosomatic Medicine*, (1947; republished in 1949 as *The New Way to Mental and Physical Health*); and *Immortal Magyar: Semmelweis, Conqueror of Childbed Fever* (1950; republished in 1962 as *Semmelweis, Conquerer of Childbed Fever.)*

GEORGE F. and
JULIAN W. SCHEER

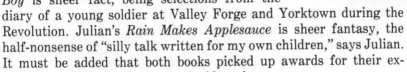

are brothers. (This picture shows Julian on the
left holding George's book, George on the right
holding Julian's.) It was mere coincidence that
each published his first juvenile on the same
day—October 30, 1964. Not so coincidentally the
brothers, reared by a father who had a large
home library, had loved books since their
childhood. Writing books of their own was
perhaps inevitable. George's *Yankee Doodle
Boy* is sheer fact, being selections from the
diary of a young soldier at Valley Forge and Yorktown during the
Revolution. Julian's *Rain Makes Applesauce* is sheer fantasy, the
half-nonsense of "silly talk written for my own children," says Julian.
It must be added that both books picked up awards for their excellence, which was also not coincidental.

George Fabian Scheer was born in Richmond, Virginia, October 21,
1917. After attending the University of Richmond, he moved to North
Carolina in 1945 and joined the University Press staff at Chapel Hill.
He remained in Chapel Hill and in 1952 became the southern
representative for a number of publishers, a literary agent, editor of a
series of books on American history, and consultant to publishers. In
Rebels and Redcoats (1957) he collaborated in editing firsthand accounts of soldiers in the Revolution. *Private Yankee Doodle* (1962) is
the adult edition of *Yankee Doodle Boy*.

Julian Weisel Scheer was born in Richmond February 20, 1926. After serving in the merchant marine during World War II, he
graduated from the University of North Carolina at Chapel Hill in
1950 and stayed there as a sportswriter. From 1953 to 1962 he was
with the *Charlotte News*. Then he joined NASA (National
Aeronautics and Space Administration) in Washington, D.C., where
he became a public affairs consultant. His first three books were
collaborations. *Tweetsie* (1958) is the history of a narrow-gauge
mountain railroad. *Choo Choo* (1958) is a biography of the Tar Heel
football player Charlie Justice. *First into Outer Space* (1959) is about
the lunar-probing missile at Cape Canaveral. Since *Upside Down Day*
(1968) Scheer has had little time for his "true love—writing." From
1971 until 1976 he and two partners operated a communications firm.
Since 1976 he has been the senior vice-president of LTV Corporation,
a Fortune 500 conglomerate, a job which entails great responsibility.

HELEN BEVINGTON

had been living in city apartments for a long time, never realizing her potential for creating poetry. When she and her husband, Dr. Merle M. Bevington, an English professor, moved to the outskirts of Durham near his classrooms at Duke University in 1942, she began writing, she says, "because of the particular pleasure of living in the country in North Carolina." Soon afterward, her delightful, witty, and sophisticated lines started appearing in the *Atlantic Monthly*, the *New Yorker*, the *Saturday Review*, and the *American Scholar*. To an interviewer she once said, "My intention is not to write serious poetry. I write verses because I enjoy and like writing, as other people play the piano, sketch, or follow other amusement."

In a memoir of her childhood, *Charley Smith's Girl* (1965), Helen Bevington tells of her youth in upstate New York, where she was born in her grandfather's Methodist parsonage. From high school she entered the University of Chicago for a degree in philosophy, then gathered a master's from Columbia with a thesis on Thoreau. While teaching at Bedford Academy she met Dr. Bevington, whom she married in 1928. He died in 1964, but Mrs. Bevington, who had returned to the classroom in 1943, is now teaching English at Duke. She writes regularly for the *New Yorker* and reviews for the *New York Times Book Review*.

Dr. Johnson's Waterfall (1946) and *Nineteen Million Elephants* (1950) are made up of poems which treat, with high humor, the things which attract and amuse her in both books and everyday life. Her third volume, *A Change of Sky* (1956), won the Roanoke-Chowan Cup and was listed by the *New York Times* among the Outstanding Books of the Year. *When Found, Make a Verse of* (1961) contains favorite quotations, original verses, and short prose comments. In 1974 she published *Beautiful Lofty People*, lighthearted essays and poems about writers and poets, and in November of that year she received the Mayflower Cup. Three autobiographical books are *The House Was Quiet and the World Was Calm* (1971), about life at Duke University between 1942 and 1956; *Along Came the Witch* (1976), her journal of the 1960s; *The Journey Is Everything, A Journal of the 1970's*, just completed. A typical Bevington verse is:

> Henry Adams once debated
> Whether or not he was educated
> It took 500 pages to give
> The answer in the negative.

BILLY GRAHAM

has, according to estimates, sold more books and has more readers than any other native North Carolinian. Because he is immediately identified as a famous evangelist the idea of Billy Graham, famous author, is surprising to many despite the millions of Graham books sold in bookstores all over the world.

William Franklin Graham was born in 1918, one of the five children of William Franklin and Morrow Coffee Graham. Young "Billy Frank" helped with chores on the family's dairy farm near Charlotte, attended Sharon High School, and showed little promise of becoming one of the most influential men of the century. Charlotte people readily recall pranks of an active, mischievous Billy Frank. Reared in a home centered on the Christian religion and church-related activities, Billy chose to study at Florida Bible Institute after his graduation from high school. He transferred to another Christian-oriented school, Wheaton College in Illinois, where he met Ruth McCue Bell, a fellow student whom he married in Montreat, North Carolina, in 1943. The Grahams have five children.

Graham was ordained in 1940 as a Methodist minister but was baptized by immersion as a Baptist before he became president in 1947 of Northwestern College in Minneapolis, Minnesota. Within a few months he decided to become a free-lance evangelist and was immediately the phenomenal force at the center of a worldwide evangelistic movement. Overnight he became an international celebrity besieged by television and radio networks, movie producers, publishing houses, and recording companies. Religious leaders and United States presidents conferred with him.

His published works developed from his sermons, but he believes his written messages, translated into many languages, will prove ultimately to be his most effective evangelism. "The books will be around long after I'm gone," he says. He spends two months of every year writing, preferably at Montreat. His wife shares his interest in writing, having had one book of her poetry published, *Sitting by My Laughing Fire* (1977).

Word Publishers

The best known of his more-than-ten published works are *Peace with God* (1954); *World Aflame* (1965); *Jesus Generation* (1971); *Angels—God's Secret Agents* (1976); and *How to be Born Again* (1977).

The Reverend Billy Graham has had conferred upon him many honorary degrees in divinity, law, literature, and the humanities.

RANDALL JARRELL

James Wommack

was a top-notch poet, essayist, and novelist when, in 1962, he wrote introductions to and translated two books of fairy tales by Ludwig Bechstein and the Brothers Grimm. The experience encouraged him to test his own inventiveness with several juvenile stories for ages eight and up. Shortly after *The Gingerbread Rabbit* (1946) came *The Bat-Poet* (1964), which received high praise and won the American Association of University Women Award for the best young people's book of the year by a North Carolinian. *The Animal Family* (1965) and *Fly by Night* (1976) are other books for young readers.

"If I were a rich man, I would pay to teach," Randall Jarrell once said. Born in Nashville, Tennessee, in 1914, he attended Vanderbilt University, then taught in several colleges before serving in World War II. After a year as a Guggenheim Fellow, he went to the University of North Carolina at Greensboro in 1947 to teach modern poetry and criticism and, as he preferred to call it, Imaginative Writing. Only a year at Princeton and two years as poetry consultant at the Library of Congress broke into his schedule of writing and teaching in Greensboro. Among his enthusiasms were Rudyard Kipling, Robert Frost, bird-watching, sports cars, and cats. He died tragically on October 14, 1965.

Recognition came quickly after his inclusion in *Five Young American Poets* (1940). From the four books of poems which followed in the next eleven years, he chose works he wished to preserve for *Selected Poems* (1955). Later books of poems and translations are *The Woman at the Washington Zoo* (1960), which won a National Book Award, and *The Lost World* (1965). Two books of essays, in which he attacks the neglect of modern poetry and defends the enigmatic nature of it, are *Poetry and the Age* (1953) and *A Sad Heart at the Supermarket* (1962). A novel which was praised for its civilized humor is *Pictures from an Institution* (1954), story of life on the campus of a progressive woman's college. Jarrell was acclaimed for his lucid translations, especially from the works of Chekhov and Rilke. Among his many prizes, honors, and grants, was his election in 1960 to membership in the National Institute of Arts and Letters.

FRED CHAPPELL

has published widely in three genres—poetry, short story, and novel. He was born on May 28, 1936, in Canton, North Carolina, the son of James and Anne Davis Chappell. At Duke University he studied under William Blackburn and after receiving a bachelor of arts degree in 1961 he remained at Duke until 1964 as an instructor in the Department of English. His college education survived interruptions when he worked with the Brown Supply Company (1957-1959) and with the Candler Furniture Company

William Blackburn

(1959-1960); during 1961 he was a proofreader for the Duke University Press. In 1959 Chappell married Susan Nicholls; they have one son, Heath. The Chappells live in Greensboro, where the author teaches at the University of North Carolina.

The plot of Chappell's first novel, *It Is Time, Lord* (1963), evolves from the hopeless psychological predicament of James Christopher, a young man trying to recapture a sense of purpose and zest in life. Three later novels include *The Inkling* (1965), which describes the strange behavior of a secluded North Carolina household; *Dagon* (1968), which also has its setting in a southern household, this time dealing with the pagan rites practiced therein; and *The Gaudy Place* (1973), which delves into the unsavory underworld in urban North Carolina. *The Gaudy Place* won the Sir Walter Raleigh Award. All four novels are in the tradition of the southern gothic, but the horror and violence symbolize an unsettled, downward-moving America in addition to depicting sensational events.

Chappell has won recognition by the National Institute of Arts and Letters and has received the Prix de Meilleur of the Academie Francaise. He is a four-time winner of the Roanoke-Chowan Cup—for *The World between the Eyes* (1971), *River: A Poem* (1975); *Bloodfire* (1978); and *Wind Mountain* (1979). In *River*, an assessment of life at age thirty-five, the poet establishes a mood of reflection by his use of water as a dominant image; there is infinite variety in form and meter. *Bloodfire* is a companion to *River*, with fire being the recurring motif and used to signify such emotions as hate, love, or anger. *Wind Mountain* (1979) is the third volume in this series on the four elements. *Earthsleep* (1980), the final volume, completes the tetralogy, the four books having the overall title *Midquest*. *Moments of Light* (1980) is a collection of Chappell's short stories.

WILMA DYKEMAN

has lived all her life near the French Broad River in the mountains of North Carolina and Tennessee. *The French Broad* (1955), one of the famous "Rivers of America" series, was completed in a year but represents a lifetime of observation and notetaking. The book is a classic. Reissued in 1965 by the University of Tennessee Press, it recounts the history, legend, biography (such as the chapter on Thomas Wolfe), sociology, and economics of a mountain region which points to this modest stream and its tributaries for its life and its ways.

Born in Asheville on May 20, 1920, Wilma was the only child of a mother whose people had lived in the North Carolina mountains since the eighteenth century. After graduating from high school and Biltmore Junior College in Asheville, the author went to Northwestern University for a bachelor's degree in speech. The summer after graduation, she met and was married to James R. Stokely, Jr., of Newport, Tennessee, a poet and writer of nonfiction. The Stokelys, who maintained homes in both Asheville and Newport, collaborated on several books. They also shared interests in collecting books and growing apples. Mr. Stokely died in 1977.

Wilma Dykeman's first writings were radio scripts and short stories, which she followed with articles for *Harper's*, the *New York Times Magazine*, *Reader's Digest*, and other periodicals. Two novels especially reflect her understanding of people in the North Carolina mountains: *The Tall Woman* (1966; now in its twentieth printing) has a strong, courageous mountain woman as its heroine; *The Far Family* (1966) is the story of a mountain family's involvement in a murder. In *Return the Innocent Earth* (1973) she made use of knowledge gleaned through her husband's association with a monolithic canning operation. *Look to This Day* (1969) is a book about her own life and convictions. In 1976 came *Tennessee: A Bicentennial History*. Recently, the writer has collaborated with her two sons on two books: with Jim Stokely on *Highland Homeland: The People of the Great Smokies* (1978) and with Dykeman Stokely on the text for *The Appalachian Mountains* (1980), a photographic study.

She is a popular lecturer and each spring teaches a course in the Department of English, University of Tennessee. Wilma Dykeman, who still writes under her maiden name, has had many honors.

58

JOHN EHLE

(pronounced EE-lee) has led a varied career, in which writing is the dominant aspect. Born in Asheville in 1925, he specialized during his high school days in writing and speech. After service in the army during World War II, he went to the University of North Carolina at Chapel Hill, where he graduated in 1949 and stayed on as teacher. Besides his short stories and books, he has been active in outdoor drama, radio, motion pictures, and television. For over two years, beginning in September, 1962, he was Governor Terry Sanford's "idea man." As special assistant to the governor, he either originated or promoted the Governor's School, the North Carolina Film Board, the Advancement School, the Learning Institute of North Carolina, the North Carolina Fund, and the North Carolina School of the Arts. Late in 1964 he resigned his professorship and with his wife went to New York. A year later he moved to Winston-Salem.

Both John Ehle's fiction and nonfiction have as their basic theme the dignity of the human being. The first of his four novels is *Move Over, Mountain* (1957), about a Negro in central North Carolina, a human entity rather than a racial symbol, who dreams of opportunity and betterment. *Kingstree Island* (1959) concerns a young outsider who faces the tyranny of a man who rules an island (obviously Ocracoke) on the North Carolina coast. *Lion on the Hearth* (1961), moving for its setting from central and eastern North Carolina, is a complex family chronicle of mountain people in a western North Carolina city. *The Land Breakers* (1964) won the Sir Walter Raleigh Award and was the selection of two book clubs; this novel of the first pioneers in the North Carolina mountains reaches its climax in a hunt for a vicious bear. After *The Road* (1967), an epic novel about the struggle to build the railroad from Old Fort to Ridgecrest in the late 1870s, *The Time of Drums* (1970), a Civil War saga, and *The Journey of August King* (1971), concerning a runaway slave girl, came an unexpected book, *The Cheeses and Wines of England and France* (1972). Ehle's interest in France was again manifested in his novel of Paris, *The Changing of the Guard* (1974).

Town and Country Studio

His marriage in 1967 to the British actress Rosemary Harris took place at his home in Penland. They have a daughter, Jennifer.

59

JONATHAN WILLIAMS

is a poet, publisher, essayist, editor, designer, and lecturer who says he lives in England "about eight months a year in a farm cottage in Dentdale in the Pennines; and [I] go back to North Carolina for the winter season to encourage students, see old friends, and pay my respects to the Great Smokies, the Galax leaves, and the Pileated Woodpecker." His hobby is hiking, so he has ample opportunity for that in both homes. Through his small but important Jargon Press, Williams has since 1951 published his own poetry and the works of other avant-garde writers and artists.

Born in Asheville on March 8, 1929, Williams was educated in local schools, attended Princeton University (1947-1949), Phillips Memorial Gallery and Atelier 17 (1950), Institute of Design in Chicago (1951), and Black Mountain College (1952-1954). He has been strongly identified with the Black Mountain group of poets who have experimented with subject matter, form, word combinations, and mood evocation. Much emphasis is placed on wit, whimsy, and the combination of visual image and words to create desired impressions. Unexpected puns, repeated syllables, and word extensions are employed, as in the beginning of "The Fall (Classic)":

tis ominous October	a world series: Ceres, also
ah, ashes, and	sere,
sere, and	seriously; a
all the old tellerian bull:	copy of the Menscheits—
	dammerung

Accompanying the poem is a photograph by Fielding Dawson of a decrepit, middle-class house on a dreary day. Understanding Williams's poetry is subordinated to hearing rhythm and pulse. His "new" poetry is the epitome of liberation and free expression. Some fifty published works include *An Ear in Bartram's Tree* (1969), *Blues and Roots/Rue and Bluets* (1971), and *The Loco Logodaedalus in Situ* (1972). Since 1954 he has given over 800 readings and lectures and has been poet-in-residence at several colleges and universities. Among many honors are a Guggenheim Fellowship for Poetry (1957-1958); six grants from the National Endowment for the Arts; an honorary degree of doctor of humane letters (1969) from Maryland's Institute of the Arts; and in 1977 the North Carolina Award in Fine Arts for a North Carolinian residing outside the state.

GUY OWEN

is a happy combination of critic, promotion man, poet, novelist, and teacher. Perhaps, like some other well-known writers, he had to leave his native state in order to see it clearly enough to write most effectively about it. True, he had produced a quantity of poems and short stories in his university days, but after four years in Florida he published his first book, *Cape Fear Country and Other Poems* (1958). Then in 1960 *Season of Fear*, a novel about a slow-witted tobacco farmer of the 1930s and the tragic prejudices and psychoses which destroy him, brought Owen to nationwide attention. After a small brochure, *The Guilty and Other Poems* (1964), came *The Ballad of the Flim-Flam Man* (1965), a comic novel in the picaresque tradition using the Cape Fear River basin as its setting. It was later made into a successful movie. Readers and viewers howled at the antics of two delightful rascals who were in business to fleece the stupid and the greedy denizens of the area. *The White Stallion and Other Poems* (1969) was followed by *Journey for Joedel* (1970), novel of a Croatan boy, and *The Flim-Flam Man and the Apprentice Grifter* (1972), sequel to the earlier novel.

Guy Owen was born in 1925 near Clarkton in Bladen County. His upbringing on a farm provided him with an abundance of raw material for later use in poetry and fiction. His undergraduate days at the university at Chapel Hill were interrupted by World War II, during which he saw duty in Germany and France. Back in Chapel Hill he completed a bachelor's degree, and followed it with an M.A. and Ph.D. in English, meanwhile teaching at Davidson and Elon colleges. From 1955 until 1961 he taught at Stetson University in Florida, then took off a year to write at Pores Knob near Moravian Falls in Wilkes County. There his "studio" in an abandoned post office provided him with the quiet he needed. In the fall of 1962 he accepted a position in the English Department at North Carolina State University and moved to Raleigh with his wife and two sons.

In addition to teaching creative writing and other courses, Professor Owen, winner of the North Carolina Award in 1971, is much concerned with contemporary southern writers. His journal, *Impetus*, was enlarged in 1964 and retitled *Southern Poetry Review*. In 1975 he relinquished editorship of this publication. With Mary C. Williams, Owen edited *Contemporary Poetry of North Carolina* in 1979.

TOM WICKER

was born in Hamlet, June 18, 1926. His undergraduate days at Chapel Hill were interrupted by a tour of duty with the navy, but he returned there to get a bachelor's degree in journalism. After graduation in 1947, he held newspaper or publicity jobs in Southern Pines; Aberdeen; Lumberton; Raleigh; Winston-Salem; Nashville, Tennessee; and Washington, D.C. For two years in the early 1950s he was a naval officer in Japan. Later he was awarded a coveted Nieman Fellowship to Harvard University. In 1959 he joined the staff of the *New York Times* in Washington, two years later became White House correspondent for it, and in 1964, at the age of thirty-eight, was named chief of the *Times*'s Washington bureau. He is now associate editor and columnist for the *Times*. He has a daughter and a son by his first marriage.

Wicker's seven novels are characterized by action, pace, suspense, a strong plot, and an economy of style. Two events in his life are not unlike something he might have put into his books. In 1957, while riverboating, he was caught in a swift current and hurled over the Great Falls of the Potomac just above Washington. Only barely bruised, he was one of the few people to escape unhurt from that experience. In Dallas on November 22, 1963, he was in the first press bus behind the open limousine in which President John F. Kennedy was riding.

Tom Wicker began his career in fiction by writing originals for the paperback market, using the pseudonym Paul Connolly. His three "Connolly" novels are *Get Out of Town* (1951), *Tears Are for Angels* (1952), and *So Fair, So Evil* (1955). The first novel using his real name was *The Kingpin* (1953), a powerful narrative of politics based on a famous senatorial campaign in North Carolina. *The Devil Must* (1957) is the character study of a man caught up in time, terror, witchcraft, and murder. Wicker thinks his best novel is *The Judgment* (1961; French title, *Sans Biscuits)*, about the destruction of complacency in

New York Times

a small southern town. *Facing the Lions* (1973) is a novel about a southern senator in Washington. Wicker's experiences during the Attica (New York) Prison riots provided material for *A Time to Die* (1975). *On Press* (1978) reflects his opinions about the current state of American journalism. A historical novel, tentatively entitled *Ol Jack*, is in progress.

62

SAM RAGAN

is, said Jonathan Daniels, "North Carolina's poet-patron of all the arts." His literary talents, interests in all things cultural, and personal achievements made Ragan the natural choice for the first secretary of the North Carolina State Department of Art, Culture, and History (now the Department of Cultural Resources) in 1972. He has supported all the arts through his newspaper column "Southern Accent," his creative writing workshops, his courses at North Carolina State University, and his many prestigious positions.

The son of William Samuel and Emma Clare Long Ragan, the poet was born in Berea, Granville County, on December 31, 1915. In 1936 he received a bachelor of arts degree from Atlantic Christian College in Wilson and soon after became editor of the *Plain Dealer*, a newspaper published in Hemp. He met his wife "during a bank robbery. Marjorie [Usher] was working for the Hamlet paper and I was in Hemp. We were both covering the same story."

Ragan in 1941 became state editor of the Raleigh *News and Observer* and until 1968 was on the staff, interrupted only by three years with the army's intelligence division during World War II. In 1968 Ragan bought the *Pilot*, a weekly newspaper in Southern Pines which he and his wife publish, writing most of the copy themselves. "Southern Accent" sometimes contains a Ragan poem along with literary criticism, anecdotes, and commentaries.

Ragan's poems evoke a romantic nostalgia and, as one critic has said, are remarkable for their freedom of line and "a starkness made poetic by concrete images." His style is characterized by *spressatura*, an art which does not reveal the exertion which the writer put into its creation. In 1963 Ragan and Thad Stem, Jr., won the Tercentenary Award for a poem they wrote together, "In the Beginning." Two books of Ragan poetry are *The Trees in the Far Pasture* (1964), for which he won the Roanoke-Chowan Award, and *To the Water's Edge* (1972). Four books written in prose have political backgrounds: *The New Day* (1964), which deals with North Carolina politics; *Dixie Looked Away* (1965); *Free Press and Fair Trial* (1967); and *Back to Beginnings: Adlai Stevenson and North Carolina* (1969), written in collaboration with Stevenson's sister, Elizabeth Stevenson Ives.

Southern Pines Pilot

63

BARBARA and
THOMAS PARRAMORE

say that when they wrote their histories of North Carolina their goal was to make history interesting. "If you have a great compilation of facts and nobody reads it, then what use is it?" asks Mrs. Parramore. Since they were writing textbooks for schoolchildren the Parramores wanted to make facts attractive by lively language and appealing illustrations. Barbara Parramore wrote *The People of North Carolina*, which has been used in the fourth grade since 1973. Her husband wrote *Carolina Quest*, which in 1978 was adopted for use in the eighth and ninth grades. In both books the unorthodox technique employed was the micro-macro approach. Each chapter begins with the story of an individual person or event, followed by a review of the background of the story and a return to the story at the end. The emphasis is often on the underdog, not the traditional hero.

Both the Parramores were well qualified to write their textbooks. Barbara Mitchell Parramore, a Guilford County native born August 29, 1932, has been a teacher and an elementary school principal; she is now associate professor and head, Department of Curriculum and Instruction, North Carolina State University. She has had published more than twenty-five articles, teachers' guides, and professional books, some of them with a coauthor or editor but most of them under her name alone. She holds a doctorate in education from Duke University and has had a host of honors, including the 1973 AAUW Award for *The People of North Carolina*.

Thomas Custis Parramore, born in Winton on December 19, 1932, was educated in North Carolina schools and holds a Ph.D. degree from the University of North Carolina at Chapel Hill. He teaches history at Meredith College but somehow finds time to write innumerable articles, many of them published in the *North Carolina Historical Review*, the *State*, *New East*, *Greenville Daily Reflector*, *Hertford County Herald*, and the *Chowan Herald*. There have been five books, including *Cradle of the Colony: The History of Chowan County and Edenton, North Carolina* (1967) and *Southampton County, Virginia* (1978).

The Parramores enjoy their two daughters, Lisa and Lynn, but somehow find time to write with commendable regularity, and both are in great demand as speakers.

WILLIAM S. POWELL

is a professor of history at the University of North Carolina, Chapel Hill, and an unchallenged authority on books written in and about North Carolina. Not surprising is that he is an editor and author himself. Born near Smithfield, April 28, 1919, he grew up and went to school in Statesville. As a boy he was curious about the past and in a notebook jotted down questions he would have asked his grandfather, a Confederate soldier, had the gentleman been living. What kind of school did he attend? what did people eat? and so on. Instead, he listened to the stock of stories his grandmother told him about events in her long life. After army service in the Pacific area, he went to Chapel Hill for bachelor's and master's degrees in history, and one in library science, then took a job at Yale University in the Rare Book Room. However, he soon returned to North Carolina to accept a position with the State Department of Archives and History in Raleigh. In 1951 he became affiliated with—and later was made curator of—the North Carolina Collection at the University of North Carolina library. A Guggenheim Fellowship in 1956 allowed him to go to England to search for facts about the men and women who had made up the Lost Colony of 1587. William Powell and his wife, Virginia, have three children.

He has served as editor of several historical and library publications, and the list of articles and pamphlets he has written is a long one. He wrote introductions for the reissue in facsimile of *The Journal of the House of Burgesses* (1749), first North Carolina printed book; and Clement Hall's *A Collection of Many Christian Experiences* ... (1783), first printed nonlegal book in North Carolina. Other publications include *North Carolina Lives* (1963), a regional "who's who"; *North Carolina: A Students' Guide to Localized History* (1965); *North Carolina* (1966), for ages ten to twelve; *The North Carolina Gazetteer* (1968), an indispensable reference; *The First State University* (1972); *Colonial North Carolina* (1972), with collaborator Hugh T. Lefler; *North Carolina: A Bicentennial History* (1977); and *John Pory, 1572-1636: The Life and Letters of a Man of Many Parts* (1977). Powell is editor of the two volumes of *The Correspondence of William Tryon and Other Selected Papers* (volume I, 1980) and the monumental multivolume *Dictionary of North Carolina Biography* (volume I, 1979).

DAPHNE ATHAS

began writing as a child and read avidly the works of such craftsmen as Dostoevski, Dickens, and Wolfe. Born in Massachusetts in May, 1924, Miss Athas was one of four children. Her mother was a New Englander and her father a native of Greece. In 1938 the family moved to Chapel Hill where Daphne attended Chapel Hill High School and then earned a bachelor's degree in 1943 at the university. Teachers Betty Smith and Phillips Russell encouraged her to write.

After graduate study at Harvard University, Miss Athas taught at Perkins Institute for the Blind at Watertown, Massachusetts. During the mid-1950s she was director of a United States service club in England, but in the early sixties she returned to the United States to work with the Massachusetts Division for the Blind. From 1967 to 1973 she lectured and taught at the University of North Carolina at Chapel Hill. Then came another year overseas, this time as Fulbright Professor of American Literature, Tehran University, Iran. In 1974 and 1979 the novelist received grants from the National Endowment for the Arts.

Although six books prior to 1979 reflect the author's background and experience, only one is truly autobiographical. The unhappiness of adolescence is the theme of *Weather of the Heart* (1947); and work experiences with the blind inspired *The Fourth World* (1956). Admittedly autobiographical is *Greece by Prejudice* (1963), in which the writer describes a visit to Greece. Winner of the Sir Walter Raleigh Award in 1971 was *Entering Ephesus*, a novel about an odd family in a southern university town (Chapel Hill, of course); it was also on the *Times* list of the year's ten best works of fiction.

Greece is the setting for *Cora* (1978), a complicated novel about a young American soldier who comes to Greece in search of his roots. When he meets Cora, a middle-aged widow, he becomes involved in a turbulent love affair and dangerous political intrigue. Imagery and symbolism are skillfully employed in developing the complex plot. *Cora* won for its author the Sir Walter Raleigh Award for 1979.

Daphne Athas has had published many short stories, articles, and poems and has collaborated on one play, *Sit on the Hearth* (1957).

BEN HAAS

was one of the most prolific writers North Carolina has produced, with his credits numbering close to a hundred. His closest competitors are Frank Slaughter and Manly Wade Wellman. Benjamin Leopold Haas, born on July 21, 1926, was one of the three sons of Otto Haas, native of Rulzheim in Alsace-Lorraine, and Lorena Jo (Michael) Haas of Mount Pleasant, North Carolina. The Haases lived in Charlotte. Otto Haas died in 1942. While he was in Central High School, Ben decided to become a writer, but he had to serve a long apprenticeship. After serving in the United States Army for two years (1945-1946) with active duty at Luzon, in the Philippines, Ben worked at several jobs, including ten years as a structural steel fabricator, the job which necessitated moving his family to Raleigh. The loss of that job literally propelled him into writing professionally.

The aspiring author now wrote even more diligently. He had enjoyed a foretaste of literary success in 1945 when he had an adventure story published by a pulp magazine; but not until 1960 did Ben Haas come into his own with the publication of *The Foragers*, a Civil War story. After that came dozens of books—some paperbacks, some hard-covers, many translated editions. At least three suspense novels, the only novel he ever wrote for juveniles—*The Troubled Summer* (1969), and many of his paperbacks, western thrillers, and short stories were published under pen names; one pseudonym was the name of his wife, Douglas Thornton. Only on his best work would the author permit "by Ben Haas" to appear on the title page.

"By Ben Haas" works include *Look Away, Look Away* (1964), a civil rights story; *The Last Valley* (1966), a tale concerned with conservation of natural resources; *The Chandler Heritage* (1972), a novel about the textile industry in the South; *Daisy Canfield* (1973), inspired by the unsolved murder of a girl in Manteo; and his final novel, *The House of Christina* (1977), a romance with its setting in Vienna, Austria. One of his three sons, Joel, who had worked with his father on other writing, helped to edit the last novel because the author had suffered a heart attack. Another attack six months later on October 27, 1977, was fatal for Ben Haas.

Jack Harmon (JAXPIX)

Margot Wilkinson

SLYVIA WILKINSON

won immediate acclaim from national literary critics and the reading public with her first novel, *Moss on the North Side*, published in 1966. *Mademoiselle* magazine (January, 1967) named the twenty-six-year-old author from Durham one of the nation's four most exciting women of the year and gave her a prestigious Merit Award. The versatile daughter of Thomas Noell and Peggy George Wilkinson displayed early talent in many areas—dancing, drama, tennis—and earned a degree in art and writing at the University of North Carolina at Greensboro. It was the poet-teacher Randall Jarrell who encouraged her to write professionally. An avid sports car enthusiast, she utilized her racing experience in *The Stainless Steel Carrot* (1971).

After earning a master's degree from Hollins, the author taught for several years—at Asheville-Biltmore College, at Stanford University, at William and Mary College, and at the University of North Carolina at Chapel Hill. In 1968-1969 she worked for the Learning Institute of North Carolina as a visiting lecturer and teacher in schools throughout the state. By 1970 she was concentrating on writing, and in 1977 when she won a Guggenheim Fellowship she was a writer-in-residence at Sweet Briar College.

Moss on the North Side was an outgrowth of Sylvia's summer visits to her grandmother's farm near Durham. The heroine is a half-Cherokee girl from the Carolina backwoods. *A Killing Frost* (1967), first of two to win Sir Walter Raleigh Awards, also has its setting in rural North Carolina, as does *Cale* (1970). *Shadow of the Mountain*, winner of the Sir Walter Raleigh Award in 1977, is set in Appalachia where a young social protester fights bravely against the poverty, ignorance, and hatred she finds in Rocky Gap. The narrative line is simple, but Wilkinson's technique in developing character is complex, with an innovative use of roman and italic type.

The author perceptively says of her own work in a letter to the editor of *Southern Living* (November, 1977) that it is possible for her to use settings other than the South but that "My characters move out of the South: they travel; I travel. But they are still Southerners. I feel comfortable with my Southern voices and those voices will keep telling my stories. . . ."

REYNOLDS PRICE

is recognized internationally as one of the most talented writers in America today. The son of William Solomon and Elizabeth Rodwell Price, the author was born in Macon, North Carolina, on February 1, 1933. The Prices lived at various times in Henderson, Asheboro, Roxboro, Warrenton, and Raleigh. Reynolds was an Angier B. Duke scholar at Duke University, a Phi Beta Kappa graduate, and a Rhodes Scholar at Merton College, Oxford University. At Broughton High School, Raleigh, his uncommon gift for writing was recognized, and at Duke he was encouraged to write by the eminent author Eudora Welty. At Merton he was praised by such literary figures as Lord David Cecil and W. H. Auden. His first published story appeared in the English *Encounter*, and subsequently a British publisher gave him a contract for a book.

A Long and Happy Life (1962), his first novel, won for Price the William Faulkner Award for a notable first novel. The material for this and later books could have come from autobiographical experiences, although the writer says his characters are "pure invention." Both of Price's parents had grown up in Warren County and to their sons Reynolds and William as well as to their parents, that area, says Price, was "home, a magnet grounded in a single place for 50 years, powered by a relay of actual lives; lives known and honored, repellent and adhesive, loved and resisted."

Later novels of Reynolds Price include *A Generous Man* (1966); *Love and Work* (1968), a short novel about a repressed English instructor; and *The Surface of Earth* (1975), a novel concerned with three generations of white North Carolinians and their black "guardians." This last book was winner of the Sir Walter Raleigh Award in 1976.

Other notable works include *The Names and Faces of Heroes* (1963), a volume of short stories; *Things Themselves* (1972), a collection of essays; *Presence and Absence: Versions from the Bible* (1973); *Early Dark* (1977), a play; *A Palpable God* (1978).

Among the many significant honors accorded Reynolds Price have been a Guggenheim Fellowship for 1964-1965, the Bellamen Foundation Award in 1972, the Lillian Smith Award in 1977, and the North Carolina Award, 1977. Since 1959 he has taught at Duke University and presently is a James B. Duke Professor of English there.

SUZANNE NEWTON

is a four-time winner of the American Association of University Women Award in juvenile literature. Her characters range from Purro, the talking cat, in *Purro and the Prattleberries* to William Thomas, teen-age practical joker in *What Are You Up To, William Thomas?* Mrs. Newton says she never writes for any particular age-group—"I just tell the story."

Suzanne Latham, daughter of Billie O'Quinn and Hannis T. Latham, Jr., was born in Bunnlevel on October 8, 1936, but grew up in Bath and Washington, in Beaufort County. After graduation from Duke University in 1957 she taught in Bladen County and continued to study music (she had studied piano since childhood) but cultivated a new pursuit, writing. Encouraged by her husband, Carl Newton, she enrolled in a correspondence course in creative writing offered by the University of Chicago. Fortunately, she had good, constructive criticism on her efforts; and by the time the Newtons moved to Raleigh in 1960 she was seriously involved with writing and in rearing a family. Her household now consists of husband Carl, four children, and family pets. Writing is a part of her carefully scheduled day.

The author's first published works were short stories and poems for adults, but her first full-length book was for children—*Purro and the Prattleberries*, AAUW Award-winner for 1971. The idea for whimsical Purro "came from my childhood memories of my brother's tom-cat Purro who had the habit of running off. To allay my brother's fears, my father used to make up adventures that Purro was having while he was away."

C/O Arnold's Corners, AAUW Award-winner for 1974, is the story of how a nonconforming twelve-year-old girl and her sedate community learn to accept each other. The hero of *What Are You Up To, William Thomas?* is a junior in high school who finds that his mischievous practical jokes can hurt as well as amuse. He must learn the hard way to fit into life with his family, teachers, and peers. Rights to produce *Reubella and the Old Focus Home* (1978), AAUW Award-winner for 1979, have been bought by Walt Disney Productions. This is an adventure story which has a serious social commentary about the elderly who still have much to give to the young. There need not be a generation gap.

70

NANCY ROBERTS

says North Carolina and the West Coast are the two most fertile fields for ghosts. She found material for a series of books about the supernatural, beginning in 1959 with *An Illustrated Guide to Ghosts & Mysterious Occurrences in the Old North State*, a collection of sixteen ghost tales with North Carolina settings. Three years later she selected nine ghost tales from South Carolina and nine from North Carolina for her book, *Ghosts of the Carolinas*. Later volumes in the series have been *This Haunted Land, Where Ghosts Still Roam* (1970); *America's Most Haunted Places* (1976); *Ghosts of the Wild West* (1976), a finalist in the Spur Awards category of best westerns for young people; and *Appalachian Ghosts* (1978). Bruce Roberts, illustrator, used trick photography in the ghost books for eerie effects. (The Robertses, then a husband-wife team, are now divorced; he is director of photography for *Southern Living* magazine.)

Mrs. Roberts was born in South Milwaukee, Wisconsin, on May 30, 1924, the daughter of Milton Lee and Maude MacRae Correll, who moved their family to New Jersey and later to Maxton, North Carolina. Nancy Correll received a B.A. degree from the University of North Carolina at Chapel Hill in 1946 and for a time owned and edited the *Scottish Chief*, a Maxton newspaper which she eventually sold, preferring to do free-lance writing.

Not all of Mrs. Roberts's writing belongs to the genre of the supernatural. *David* (1968), is a heartrending, warm account of the author's experiences with her little son, a mongoloid. To even things up for her daughter, Nancy Lee, Mrs. Roberts wrote *Sense of Discovery: The Mountain*, about Nancy Lee's adventures on Grandfather Mountain.

Later books using North Carolina material have included *Where Time Stood Still: A Portrait of Appalachia*, selected by the *New York Times* as one of the outstanding children's books of 1970; *The Governor* (1972), a documentary depicting Governor Robert W. Scott in routine, everyday action; and *The Goodliest Land: North Carolina* (1973), a potpourri of tales about places, people, history, and ghosts. Most have been illustrated by Bruce Roberts.

Jeep Hunter

Nancy Roberts has had brief business ventures and in February, 1972, became the first woman ever to file as candidate for governor of North Carolina. She withdrew a week later, but the brief candidacy made history.

DORIS BETTS

was born in Statesville, June 4, 1932. In high school her special interest was journalism, and she sent news reports in to various newspapers under her maiden name, Doris Waugh. In 1950 she entered the University of North Carolina at Greensboro, took a job in the campus news bureau, contributed to the college newspaper and magazine, and still managed to make straight A's in her studies. Among her teachers was Frances Gray Patton, distinguished writer from Durham. During her sophomore year Doris married Lowry M. Betts of Columbia, South Carolina, but she did not give up her college career.

In 1954 Doris Betts moved to Chapel Hill where her husband was a law student and where Mrs. Betts somehow studied, wrote, held down a job, and had her first child. (There are now three Betts children.) The family moved to Sanford in 1957 when Mr. Betts began his practice of law, and in the following year Doris received a Guggenheim Fellowship. Mrs. Betts is now a professor of English at the University of North Carolina at Chapel Hill. She also contributes regularly to several newspapers in the area and in 1962 was named editor of the weekly *Sanford News-Leader*. In addition, she still writes stories for such popular periodicals as *Redbook* and *Woman's Day*.

Three of her books have earned for their author the Sir Walter Raleigh Award. Her first novel, *Tall Houses in Winter* (1958) was a winner. In it she uses a flashback technique to tell the story of a native who returns from the North to Stoneville, her fictional name for Statesville, and of the conflicts which develop. *The Scarlet Thread* (1965), winner two, is a novel about two brothers and their sister in a rural textile-mill community in piedmont North Carolina during the period 1898-1900. Winner three was *Beasts of the Southern Wild* (1973), a collection of short stories. *The Gentle Insurrection and Other Stories* (1954), winner of the UNC Putnam Prize, is a collection of character studies which depict various southern people who are isolated and lonely. Another collection of stories is *The Astronomer and Other Stories* (1966). *The River to Pickle Beach* (1972) is a novel of murder and violence on the North Carolina coast. Another novel is almost ready for publication in 1981.

One of Doris Betts's most prestigious honors came in 1975 when she received the North Carolina Award.

HEATHER ROSS MILLER

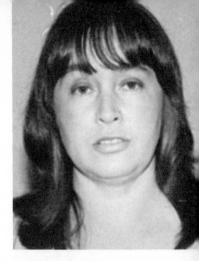

is the youngest of a family often spoken of with great respect as the "writing Rosses." Her father, Fred Ross, and her uncle, James Ross, have novels to their credit. Her aunt, Eleanor Ross Taylor, wife of the acclaimed writer, Peter Taylor, concentrates on poetry; and another aunt, Jean Justice, wife of poet Donald Justice, is a writer of short stories. So far, Heather Ross Miller has published four novels, two volumes of poetry, and a collection of short stories.

Born in Badin in Stanly County in 1940, Heather Ross won a prize for poetry when she was sixteen. While earning a bachelor of arts degree and a master's at the University of North Carolina at Greensboro, she concentrated on writing and studied with Randall Jarrell. Before she graduated, the aspiring young writer married Clyde H. Miller, a state forester. Five books were produced during the Millers' twelve years of residency in Bladen County. Since 1975 the family, which now includes son Kirk and daughter Melissa, has been back in Badin on Elm Street.

Mrs. Miller presently teaches creative writing at Pfeiffer College. She has found numerous opportunities to encourage other ambitious writers. It has been possible for her to travel in Europe through fellowships—there have been two from the National Endowment for the Arts and in 1979 there was a prestigious United States-United Kingdom Exchange Fellowship.

The Miller novels, often in the southern gothic tradition, have autobiographical overtones and settings recognizable by Stanly County people. *The Edge of the Woods* (1964) portrays a heroine whose life and mental stability were almost destroyed by her malevolent, domineering grandfather. *Tenants of the House* (1966), set in Jonesboro (Badin), depicts the life of residents in an apartment house who are modern approximations of mythical and Biblical figures. This book won the Sir Walter Raleigh Award for 1966. *Gone a Hundred Miles* (1968) was inspired by the life of an early German doctor in Stanly County. *Confessions of a Champeen Fire Baton Twirler* is a humorous novel of adolescence, published in 1976.

The Wind Southerly (1967), a collection of thirty-one poems, won the Oscar Arnold Young Memorial Cup; *Horse Horse Tyger Tyger*, a second volume of verse, was published in 1973. Later publications are *A Spiritual Divorce and Other Stories* (1974) and *A Shooting Gallery* (1976).

RICHARD WALSER

is the author of this PICTUREBOOK, one of the many volumes and
pamphlets and articles he has prepared on North Carolina writers
and writing.

Born in Lexington in 1908, he grew up in a home where his father
was a collector of North Carolina books. After a freshman year at
Davidson, he went to the university at Chapel Hill and spent much
time in the special room of North Caroliniana at the library. Following his graduation he began teaching English at Linwood High School
and went on from there to Lexington, Durham, and Greenville. Then
the war came, and he served as a naval officer in the Southwest
Pacific and Panama. He is now a commander, U.S.N.R. (Ret.) After
the war he taught at Chapel Hill for a year, then transferred to North
Carolina State University at Raleigh, where from 1946 until his
retirement in 1970 he was a teacher in the Department of English. He
received a Guggenheim Fellowship in 1957 and the North Carolina
Award in 1976.

North Carolina Poetry (1941) was based on a notion that Tar Heels
would like a book of verse by their own poets. Thereafter followed
several other anthologies, then short studies of Inglis Fletcher, Bernice Kelly Harris, and Thomas Wolfe. *The Enigma of Thomas Wolfe*
(1953) was one of the first of the now-popular books containing essays
about one figure by numerous writers. In modern facsimile editions,
Walser reissued the first North Carolina book of poetry, James Gay's
1810 *Collection of Various Pieces . . . Chiefly Patriotic* (1964); the first
North Carolina play, Lemuel Sawyer's 1824 *Blackbeard* (1952); and
the first North Carolina novel, Robert Strange's 1839 *Eoneguski*
(1960; see page 6 of this PICTUREBOOK). In 1961 he edited *The Poems
of Governor Thomas Burke of North Carolina* from eighteenth-
century manuscripts (see page 3). His *North Carolina Miscellany*
(1962) is an assortment of odd information on places, people, inci-

dents, and folklore. In *North Carolina Parade*
(1966) he collaborated with Julia Montgomery
Street in writing a book for young people about
Tar Heels from earliest times until the mid-
1960s.

For other titles, see inside back cover.

74